CHRISTIAN ETHICS,

OR

THE SCIENCE OF DUTY.

BY

JOSEPH ALDEN, D. D., LL. D.,

LATE PRESIDENT OF JEFFERSON COLLEGE. AUTHOR OF "ELEMENTS OF INTELLECTUAL PHILOSOPHY," "THE SCIENCE OF GOVERNMENT," ETC., ETC.

NEW YORK:

IVISON, PHINNEY, BLAKEMAN & Co.,

Nos. 48 & 50 WALKER STREET.

CHICAGO: S. C. GRIGGS & Co.

1866.

Stereotyped by SMITH & McDOUGAL, 82 & 84 Beekman St., N. Y.

TO

EDWARD SMITH,

MERCHANT, OF NEW YORK.

DEAR SIR:—

The opportunities for observation which our long and intimate friendship has furnished, have wrought in me a conviction that the principles inculcated in this volume have guided you in your business transactions and social relations. Those who succeed in acquiring wealth by acting on such principles, confer a moral as well as pecuniary benefit on the public. Men of this class are among the most efficient teachers of morality. Believing you to belong to this class, I take the liberty of inscribing to you this volume, as a mark of my respect and affection.

JOSEPH ALDEN.

PREFACE.

THE author designed to write a text-book—not a commentary. He has attempted to furnish a directory of duty; but in so doing, he has not enumerated all the duties of men in all the relations in which they may be placed. He has selected such principles and rules as will readily guide the honest inquirer into all truth in relation to duty.

The work is emphatically a practical one, yet the author has not been guilty of the folly of attempting to separate the practical from the theoretical. They are united in every mind. Every one has a reason, sound or unsound, for the rule he adopts. To give the reason for a rule is to give the theory of it.

The reasons of the duties set forth are stated, except in cases where they can be readily inferred. A book which leaves nothing for the teacher and pupil to think out, must needs be a dull one.

Truths expressed in technical language and in scientific forms, are less likely to become incorporated with the thinking of the student than when expressed in ordinary language, and illustrated by familiar objects. A treatise on Ethics should be a directory of life: it will be influential in forming the character, in proportion as its principles become incorporated with the mind, and the form and arrangement are forgotten.

Among the friends of morality, there is not much diversity of opinion as to duties. There are differences with respect to the religious theory of certain duties. In such cases, the authority for the duty has been given in the language of Scripture, and the theological explanation left with the teacher. The author has thus not omitted any important duty, and has avoided giving to his work a sectarian character. No believer in the Bible will find in this work any principle to which he can object. He may differ from the author in his application of principles.

The Bible is appealed to throughout as authority in all matters of duty. Its authority is admitted by all Christians, however diverse may be their theological views.

A deep impression of the importance of moral culture is felt in the community. It is seen that intelligence alone will not execute justice, and maintain truth. The pervading influence of moral principle is the only substitute for the bayonet. Hence the author trusts that this attempt to furnish an aid for the moral education of the young will not be looked upon with disfavor.

NEW YORK, *June* 1, 1866.

CONTENTS.

CHAPTER VI.

CHAPTER VII.

CHAPTER VIII.

CHAPTER IX.

CHAPTER X.

CHAPTER IX.

CHAPTER XII.

CHAPTER XIII.

CHAPTER XIV.

CHAPTER XV.

CHAPTER XVI.

CHAPTER XVII.

CHAPTER XVIII.

CHAPTER XIX.

CHAPTER XX.

CHAPTER XXI.

CHAPTER XXII.

CHAPTER XXIII.

CHAPTER XXIV.

CHRISTIAN ETHICS.

CHAPTER I.

RIGHT AND WRONG—CONSCIENCE—MORAL OBLIGATION.

Every one possessed of common sense knows that there is a difference between right and wrong, as truly as he knows that there is a difference between black and white. He knows that there are some things which ought to be done, and some things which ought not to be done. He knows that he ought to do right, and that he ought not to do wrong. He knows what duty is. He may not know what his duty is in all cases, and he may not do it when he does know it; but he knows what duty is.

If the question be asked, how do we know that there is a difference between right and wrong? it may be replied, that we know it in the same way that we know there is a difference between truth and error. How do we know that some things are true and some things false? We see them to be true or false, that is, the mind sees that they are true or false. How do we know that two and two make four? That two things equal to a third thing are equal to one another? that the whole of a thing is greater than a part of it? The mind sees the truth of these propositions as soon as they are set before it. When truths are thus directly perceived, they are said to be intuitively perceived. They are called intuitive truths.

If it be asked in regard to any one of these propositions, or in regard to any self-evident proposition, *in what does this truth consist?* No answer can be given. It may be said that it consists in being true; but that answer conveys no information. It simply re-affirms the truth of the proposition. If it be asked, *why is it true?* No answer can be given. It may be said, "*because it is true;*" but that is simply re-affirming its truth. It may be said, "*on account of the nature of things;*" but that expression, if it have any meaning, simply re-affirms the truth of the proposition.

If it be asked, how do we know that some things are right? The reply is, we see them to be right, that is, the mind sees that they are right. You see a man rescue another from drowning: you see that the action is right: you see that the neglect to rescue him, if within one's power, would be wrong.

You see a man returning money entrusted to him for safe keeping: you see that the action is right: you see that a refusal to return it, without just cause, would be wrong. These actions are intuitively perceived to be right.

If it be asked, why they are right, and in what their rightness consists? no answers can be given. We cannot tell why a proposition relating to duty intuitively perceived is right, or in what its rightness consists, any more than we can tell why an intuitive truth is true, and in what its truth consists.

Perhaps some may say, it is right to rescue a drowning man, because it is an act of benevolence. It may then be asked, why is an act of benevolence right? The only reply that can be given is, "because it is right," and that, as we have seen in regard to truth, is simply re-affirming the proposition.

Some say an act of benevolence is right, because it tends to promote human happiness: but then it may be asked, why is it right to promote happiness? In the end, we are shut up to the answer, "because it is right," that is, to an intuitive perception of right.

Some truths, like the examples given above, are perceived intuitively, and some are arrived at by reasoning. For example, you see footprints on the sand, and you infer that some person has been there. You see a person habitually partaking of intoxicating drinks, and you infer that his health will suffer. In these and similar cases, you see some things to be true, because you have seen certain other things to be true.

The truth of a proposition often depends upon the truth of several other propositions, and we must know the truth of those propositions before we can know its truth. The truth of this remark is plain, especially to those who have any acquaintance with geometry.

In like manner, while some duties are intuitive, there are others which are arrived at by reasoning. Our perception of the rightness of an action may depend upon our perception of several, perhaps many, things connected with it.

When our perception of a truth relating to politics depends upon our perception of several other truths, we are liable to error. So, also, when our perception of a truth relating to duty depends upon our perception of several other truths, we are liable to error. We are as liable to make mistakes in our perceptions in regard to duty, as in our perceptions in regard to politics, or law. The human mind is not infallible in its reasonings on any subject. It may err even in its mathematical reasonings.

The mind was made to know truth relating to duty as truly as it was made to know truth relating to agriculture, or commerce, or legislation. Its mode of proceeding in regard to all kinds of truth is the same. In regard to all kinds of truth, some truths are perceived intuitively, and others are arrived at by reasoning: in other words, some truths are perceived immediately, by simply looking at them, and others mediately, or by the aid of other truths.

It may be asked, Does not conscience make known

to us our duty? Yes, but you must understand what is meant by conscience. Conscience is not an agent dwelling in the mind, and issuing its commands or dictates. Conscience is defined to be the power by which the mind perceives the difference between right and wrong. But a power of the mind is not something separate from the mind. When we speak of the mind as having certain powers or faculties, we mean that the mind can do certain things. When the mind perceives external objects through the agency of the senses, it is said to be exercising the faculty of perception. When the mind recalls past events, it is said to be exercising the faculty of memory. When the mind perceives truths, by means of other truths, it is said to be exercising the reasoning faculty. When the mind perceives duty, it is said to be exercising the moral faculty, or conscience. The expressions, "conscience makes known to us our duty," and "the mind perceives duty," have the same meaning. The first form of expression is figurative, the second is literal. We are much less liable to error, when we use literal, than when we use figurative expressions.

When it is said that conscience is an original attribute of our nature, the meaning is, that the human mind was made with the power of perceiving right and wrong. When it is said that conscience is fallible, the meaning is, the mind may make mistakes as to duty.

Some writers have attempted to *prove* that we ought to do right. They have never succeeded. It is impossible to prove a self-evident truth; because, no truth more evident can be brought to support it. We should do what is right because it is right. The obligation to do right is involved in the perception of right. To perceive what is right in our sphere of action, is to be under obligation to do it. We might as well ask, why should we believe what is true? as, why should we do what is right?

Evil consequences may follow the belief of error; but that is not the reason why we should believe truth. A true proposition should be believed because it is true. A right action should be performed because it is right.

CHAPTER II.

MORAL NATURE OF MAN—MAN A FREE AGENT—CLAIMS OF DUTY PARAMOUNT—REVELATION NEEDED.

The phrase, "our moral nature," is often met with, especially in treatises on duty. When it is said, our moral nature requires us to act in a certain manner, the meaning is, we, that is, our minds perceive it to be our duty to act in that manner.

By our moral nature is meant our capacity to perceive duty, and to act freely in view of it. We know that we can perceive duty; we know that we are free agents.

The proposition, "Man is a free moral agent," is a self-evident truth. No objections to it are of any weight. Whether we can answer them or not, we know that we are free to do right or wrong, and hence are worthy of blame when we do wrong.

Suppose objections that you could not answer were brought to the proposition, "The whole is greater than its part?" It would not in the least shake your belief of that proposition: so if objections that you cannot answer are brought to the proposition, "Man is a free moral agent," they will not in the least shake your belief of that proposition.

Duty has higher claims upon us than anything else has. An action may be adapted to give us a great deal of pleasure ; yet, if it is not right, it must not be performed. Suppose some fine strawberries are before you. It would be very pleasant to eat them ; but they do not belong to you. The claims of duty are higher than the claims of pleasure.

An action may be adapted to promote our pecuniary interest ; yet, if it is not right, it must not be performed. A man puts into your hands a large sum of money for safe keeping. He dies and no one knows that you have it. You might purchase a fine house with it ; but it is not yours. It belongs to the heirs of the man who placed it in your hands. Duty requires you to deliver it to them. The claims of duty are higher than the claims of interest.

That which is right is always to be done. There is no exception to this rule. It is never right to do wrong. Nothing can excuse us for doing wrong. Hence, the knowledge of duty is the most important of all knowledge.

We have seen that the mind perceives some duties directly and others indirectly, or by means of reasoning. We have seen that the mind is liable to err in reasoning. In complicated circumstances, it is often difficult to find the truth—difficult to learn what our duty is. Hence we need aid, in order to arrive at a perfect knowledge of duty. We need aid from One who cannot err. We need aid from our Heavenly Father. In order to a perfect science of duty—a perfect system of morals—a perfect directory of life, we need the aid of Divine Revelation.

This will further appear, when we consider that, without the aid of revelation, we in many cases arrive at a knowledge of duty, by observing the consequences of actions. We see a white powder resembling sugar. We do not know whether it would be right for us to take it or not. There is nothing in the action directly viewed that will enable us to determine whether the act of taking it would be right or wrong. The decision depends upon a consideration of consequences. When we learn that the powder is poisonous, we know that it would be wrong to take it, or to administer it to others. Knowledge acquired by personal experience would necessarily come too late.

There are many things in practical life, in relation to which, without the aid of revelation, a knowledge of duty could be acquired only by a consideration of their consequences.

Our knowledge of right and wrong ought not in any case to depend upon experiment, since that would expose us to the liability of doing wrong. As it is our duty always to do right, we ought to avoid that liability. We need in all cases to know our duty at the outset. Hence we need directions from One who knows all things. We need directions from God.

We cannot, by the exercise of our natural faculties arrive at a perfect knowledge of duty, even in regard to those things which are within reach of our natural faculties. But we have duties which are entirely beyond the reach of our natural faculties—duties of which our unaided minds could not acquire even a partial and imperfect knowledge. There are made known to us in the Bible, truths respecting God, which the unaided human mind could never discover. From those truths arise certain duties. A knowledge of those truths is necessary to a knowledge of duties grounded upon them.

A consideration of those truths would lead us into the domain of Natural Theology. Allusion is made to them to show that the teachings of the Bible are necessary to a perfect knowledge of duty.

The teachings of the Bible include and sanction all the duties which the human mind can reach without its aid, and add others peculiarly its own. The teachings of nature and revelation are always harmonious; but the latter corrects and enlarges the former. In attempting to give a complete enumeration of our duties, we shall have recourse to both sources of knowledge.

Every one should desire to know his whole duty that he may do it. He who is willingly ignorant of a portion of his debts that he may not pay them, is not honest toward men. He who is willingly ignorant of some of his duties that he may not do them, is not honest toward God.

Happiness is connected with the performance of duty, and unhappiness with the violation or neglect of it. God has so ordained. Happiness is incidental to the performance of duty. The true way to secure it, is to make the performance of duty our first object.

The order and well-being of the state depend upon the performance of duty on the part of its citizens. If all the citizens of a state were to perform all their duties, that state would speedily reach the highest degree of prosperity.

Attempts have been made to construct the science of duty without the aid of revelation : in other words, attempts have been made to show that a perfect system of duty can be taught without having recourse to the Bible. Such attempts have failed. We have seen the causes of the failure. We have seen that we may err in our perceptions of duty even on subjects within the compass of our powers. We have seen that there are some duties which we owe to ourselves and to others, which, as they are learned from consequences, could not be learned in time for action. We have seen that there are some duties to God, which are founded on knowledge concerning him which the light of nature does not furnish.

Some writers on moral philosophy, though sincere Christians, have seemed reluctant to be under obligations to the Bible. The astronomer is not reluctant to avail himself of the aid of the telescope. The moralist should not be reluctant to avail himself of the aid of light from above. If it is the object of a writer to see how far the unaided mind can go in learning duty, he will of course confine himself to the teachings of nature; but if his object is to set forth a complete system of duty, he will of course avail himself of the aid of the omniscient One, when that aid is placed within his reach.

CHAPTER III.

DIVISION OF DUTIES—DUTY TO GOD INCLUDES ALL DUTY—THE STUDY OF HIS CHARACTER—PROVIDENCE—OBEDIENCE AND REVERENCE.

The existence of God is taught by nature and by the Bible, or rather it is taught by nature and assumed by the Bible. The Bible does not begin by saying "there is a God," but by saying, "in the beginning God created the heavens and the earth."

The arguments from nature for the existence of God, belong to the science of Natural Theology, and will not be given in this work. The Bible affirms that nature teaches the existence of God. "For the invisible things of Him from the creation of the world are clearly seen, being understood by the things that are made, even his eternal power and Godhead." Rom., i. 20.

Our duties to God include all other duties. The duties which we owe to men, we owe also to God. For example, to treat our neighbor kindly is a duty which we owe to him. It is also a duty which we owe to God.

Our duties are commonly divided into, 1. Those which we owe to God, 2. Those which we owe to ourselves, 3. Those which we owe to others.

If we do our whole duty to God, we shall necessarily do our duty to ourselves and to others. To do our whole duty to God, is to do all his will. It is his will that we should do what is termed our duty to ourselves and to others.

The proposition, "It is our duty to do the will of God," thus includes all our duties. We need then to know what that will is—what God would have us do in the varied relations of life. We need to consider duty in detail. To this we shall now proceed.

It is our duty to study the character of God as it is made known to us by his word and by his works.

God is our Father. Christ has told us to call him "Our Father." It is fitting that the child should know the character of his father, especially when that character is one of infinite excellence.

A knowledge of God's character is necessary in order that we may know the duties we owe him. For example, we need to know that he is just, that we may see it to be our duty to submit to his government. We need to know that he is merciful, that we may see it to be our duty to ask pardon for our sins. We need to know that he is infinitely lovely, that we may see it to be our duty to love him with all the heart.

The study of the divine character has a tendency to promote the perfection of our own character. Experience shows that we become like those whose characters are the object of our admiring study. The more we study, in a proper manner, the character of God, the more we shall be like him. The Apostle recognizes this truth. He says that those "beholding as in a glass, the glory of the Lord, are changed into the same image from glory to glory, even, as by the Spirit of the Lord. 2 Cor., iii. 18.

There is no study so glorious, so exalting as the study of the character of God,—"the high and lofty One that inhabiteth eternity, whose name is Holy." Isa., lvii. 15.

It is our duty to recognize God's hand in his works. "All things were made by him, and without him was not any thing made that was made." John, i. 3. Through the agency of second causes, he is still carrying on his operations in nature. "Who covereth the heaven with clouds, who prepareth rain for the earth, who maketh grass to grow upon the mountains." Ps. cxlvii. 8. "He giveth snow like wool: he scattereth the hoar frost like ashes." Ps. cxlvii. 16. "Thou hast made summer and winter." Ps. lxxiv. 17. "My Father worketh hitherto." John, v. 17. We are thus in the midst of the works of God, and he is constantly at work around us—guiding the stars, causing the seasons to return, weaving the leaf, painting the flower and ripening the fruit.

We should not live in the midst of these wonderful works and operations forgetful of their Author.

Sir Christopher Wren built St. Paul's church in London. Suppose his son should visit that edifice, and admire its beauties, without once thinking of his father! Suppose the daughters of Milton should read and admire Paradise Lost without thinking of their blind old father who wrote it! They would do what multitudes of God's children do. They are surrounded by his handy-work. On one side there is the exhibition of stupendous power: on the other, specimens of exquisite skill: here is an example of his provident care for the wants of his children, and there are intimations of his inflexible regard for law, and yet they notice none of these things. "God goeth by them and they see him not." They may wonder and admire, but "God is not in all their thoughts."

We should form the habit of associating thoughts of God, grateful and adoring thoughts, with his works. There is truth as well as poetry in the following passage from Cowper.

"He looks abroad into the varied field
Of nature, and, though poor, perhaps, compared
With those whose mansions glitter in his sight,
Calls the delightful scenery all his own

His are the mountains and the vallies his,
And the resplendent rivers. His t' enjoy
With a propriety that none can feel
But who, with filial confidence inspired,
Can lift to heaven an unpresumptuous eye
And smiling say, 'My Father made them all.'"

It is our duty to recognize God's hand in his providential government. We do not live in a fatherless and ungoverned world. "His kingdom ruleth over all." Ps. ciii. 19. "The Most High ruleth in the kingdom of men, and giveth it to whomsoever he will." Dan., iv. 17. "Promotion cometh neither from the east nor from the west nor from the south. But God is the judge: he putteth one down, and setteth up another." Ps. lxxv. 6. "Affliction cometh not forth of the dust, neither doth trouble spring out of the ground." Job, v. 6. "Whom the Lord loveth he chasteneth and scourgeth every son whom he receiveth." Heb., xii. 6. "Who worketh all things after the counsel of his own will." Eph., i. 11.

God governs nature by fixed, uniform laws. He has made men free agents. In a way unknown to us, but neither by miraculous agency nor by infringing on man's freedom, he exerts a controlling influence over all events.

This controlling Providence should be at all times recognized. The neglect of this duty is thus rebuked by the Apostle, "Go to, now, ye that say, to-day or to-morrow we will go into such a city, and continue there a year, and buy and sell and get gain : for that ye ought to say, if the Lord will, we shall live and do this or that." James, iv. 13.

We cannot see *how* God can control all things without interfering with the operation of the laws of nature, or with human freedom. This does not disprove the fact that he does so. The fact is established, as we have seen, by his own testimony.

It is our duty to render implicit obedience to God's commands. We should obey him because it is right to obey him. His commands are the expression of his will. His will is always right. It is as impossible for his will to be wrong as it is for him to lie ; "It was impossible for God to lie." Heb., vi. 18. We have seen that we were made to do right : consequently we were made to obey God.

We should obey him because he is our Creator, Benefactor, and Father, and is possessed of every conceivable perfection. The creature belongs to the creator. Of course, the creator has a right to govern the creature according to the nature given him. "Shall the thing formed say to him that formed it, why hast thou made me thus?" Rom., ix. 20.

We are dependent upon our Benefactor for life and all things. We ought to do the righteous will of him on whom we are thus dependent. Children should do the will of their wise and loving Father.

The fact that God will punish disobedience, is not

the ground of our obligation to obey him. That obligation is founded upon his character and the relations we sustain to him. It is not proper to say, "we must obey God, because he will punish us if we do not." To conform to his will through fear of punishment is not obedience. It is an act of prudence rather than an act of obedience. At least, it is not the obedience he requires. He requires a cordial obedience—loyalty of heart.

It is our duty to do God's will at all times and in all circumstances. To disregard his will is to do wrong. It can never be right for us to do wrong. God requires perfect obedience. We are to "have respect unto all his commandments." Ps. cxix. 6. The New Testament does not lower God's claims to our obedience. "Be ye therefore perfect, even as your Father which is in heaven is perfect." Matt., viii. 48.

Some seem to think that doing "pretty nearly right," will suffice. But we were made to do right and nothing else. Whenever we see that a thing is wrong, we know that we ought not to do it. Our moral nature makes no exceptions in favor of some acts of wrong doing. It does not decide that little sins are not wrong. It requires us to avoid everything that is wrong. Thus the voice of our moral nature is in unison with the voice of God, when it requires perfect obedience.

It is our duty to cherish feelings of reverence towards God. The fear of the Lord which is the beginning of wisdom, and which is so much insisted on in the Bible, is not a servile fear, but profound reverence. The Scriptures describe the angelic hosts as exhibiting the deepest reverence towards God. Isa., vi. 2. Rev., iv. 8. He commands us "to reverence his sanctuary." Lev., xix. 30. The apostle Paul defines acceptable service to be that "accompanied with reverence and godly fear." The first petition in the Lord's prayer, refers to this duty: "Hallowed be thy name."

Reverence is a feeling which the holy character of God is adapted to inspire. God makes no arbitrary requirements. His commands are always in the highest degree reasonable. When he commands us to reverence him, he simply commands us to exercise that feeling which his character rightly viewed is adapted to awaken in pure and loyal minds. Such minds we are under obligation to have.

Some human characters are so pure and august as to awaken reverence. Who does not reverence the characters of John Jay and George Washington? If we reverence the characters of men, much more should we reverence the character of God.

Reverence will lead us to avoid not only all profanity but all light and irreverent use of the names of God. It is said that Sir Isaac Newton always made a reverential pause before pronouncing the name of God.

There are forms of expression in somewhat common use, which savor of irreverence and should be avoided. The exclamations, Gracious! Mercy! Goodness! and the like, are abridged expressions in which the name of God originally occurred. They may be regarded as elliptical oaths and should therefore be avoided.

Reverence will lead us to avoid all trifling with sacred things, all levity and indecorum in connection with the public worship of God, all sportive allusions to solemn religious facts, all ludicrous applications of passages of Scripture.

A religious character in which reverence is lacking is very defective, if it be not radically unsound. A burning zeal, and great apparent devotion to works of benevolence, will not atone for the want of reverence which is the natural result of right views of the divine character.

CHAPTER IV.

LOVE TO GOD—CONFIDENCE IN HIS TESTIMONY, PROMISES, AND CHARACTER—REASONABLENESS OF FAITH.

It is our duty to love God. "Thou shalt love the the Lord thy God with all thy heart, and with all thy thy soul, and with all thy might." Deut., vi. 3. Christ declares this to be "the first and great commandment." Matt., xxii. 38.

To love God with all the heart and soul and might, is to love him supremely, and as intensely as the constitution of our nature will allow.

Throughout the Scriptures, the duty of loving God is set forth with great variety of expression. Love is said to be "the fulfilling of the law." Rom., xiii. 10.

When it is said that love is the fulfilling of the law, the meaning is not that the exercise of the emotion or affection of love is a substitute for the various actions required by the law: the meaning is, that when one loves God supremely, love will spontaneously prompt him to do all God's will. The sense of obligation will be merged in love.

The affectionate child loves to do his parent's will. Obedience is rendered not from fear, nor out of regard to authority, but from love. Such should be the relation of the soul to God.

Our obligation to love God is founded on the infinite excellence of his character, and on the relations he sustains to us. God is holy. "I, the Lord your God, am a holy God." Lev., xix. 2. Holiness embodies all moral perfection. "As your Father which is in heaven is perfect." Matt., v. 48.

All who admit the existence of God, agree in ascribing to him all possible perfection. He is infinite in knowledge, wisdom, justice, goodness, and truth : in other words, he is infinitely lovely.

If he were not infinitely lovely, we could not be under obligation to love him with all the heart. We were made to love excellence, and nothing else.

Hence, when God commands us to love him with all the heart, the command is not an arbitrary one. He simply tells us to exercise our hearts—our emotive natures, as they were made to be exercised. If he were to tell us to admire the rainbow or the star-lit sky, he would tell us to do a very natural thing ; for we were made to admire beauty. So also we were made to love excellence. The command to love God with all the heart is in perfect keeping with the original constitution of the human mind, and the character of God.

Our obligation to love God rests also on the relations he sustains to us. He is our Heavenly

Father, and all his acts towards us are in keeping with that relation. The father who performs all his duties towards his child, is worthy of love and honor.

God "giveth us richly all things to enjoy." 1 Tim., vi. 17. "Like as a father pitieth his children, so the Lord pitieth them that fear him." Ps. ciii. 13. "God so loved the world that he gave his only begotten Son, that whosoever believeth in him should not perish, but have everlasting life." John, iii. 16.

Thus, from the relations he sustains to us, and the manner in which he has treated us, we are bound to love him. We should love him, "because he first loved us." 1 John, iv. 19.

To love is to be happy. To love with all the heart a perfect object is to be perfectly happy. When God commands us to love him with all the heart, he is simply commanding us to be as happy as the constitution of our nature will permit.

Love is not voluntary. We cannot love any one by willing to do so. Our control over our affections is an indirect control. We can awaken love by contemplating truths adapted to produce it, just as we awaken the emotion of beauty by contemplating objects adapted to awaken it.

It is our duty to have confidence in God—in his declarations, his promises, and in his character.

We should implicitly believe his testimony. The

Bible contains his testimony to many truths that reason cannot reach. A large part of our knowledge in respect to God and a future life is gained from the testimony of God. We put full confidence in the testimony of such a man as Washington. If we can thus put full confidence in the witness of man, "the witness of God is greater." John, v. 9.

We are not required to believe without evidence, that the Bible contains the testimony of God—that the Bible is the word of God. It must first be proved that the Bible is the word of God. This being proved, it is reasonable to believe everything it contains, because it is impossible for God to lie.

The evidence that the Bible is the word of God is abundant. To set forth that evidence does not come within the scope of this work. There are many able treatises on the subject.

The fact that we may not be able fully to comprehend a proposition, is no reason for not believing it, provided it rests on the testimony of God. An astronomer may make a statement to a child. The child may be unable to understand it, but has no right to reject it as false.

We must distinguish between the incomprehensible and the contradictory and absurd.

It is our duty to exercise perfect reliance upon the promises of God. There are some men on whose promises we rely. Our reliance is founded upon a knowledge of their characters. Our reliance upon God's promises is founded upon a knowledge of his character. We know that he is true and unchangeable and omnipotent. Hence his promises will surely be performed. All distrust of God's promises dishonors him. It is practically charging him with falsehood. You would consider it an insult to distrust the promise of a perfectly honorable man. What is it to distrust the promises of the God of truth?

Many of God's promises to us are conditional. If we fail to receive the blessings promised, it is because we fail to meet the required conditions.

We should have perfect confidence in the character of God, that is, we should have perfect faith in God. This will cause us to feel perfectly sure that all that he does is wise, and just, and good.

A wise parent often does things which his child does not and cannot understand. The child should not call in question the wisdom and kindness of his parent. He should have confidence in him.

The infinitely wise and holy God does many things which we do not understand. We should not call in question his wisdom or goodness. We should have perfect confidence in him. We should feel perfectly sure that all he does is right, whether we can see it to be so or not.

To have confidence in God is to have faith in God.

Faith is not something distinct from reason—something opposed to reason. It is the most reasonable of all things. What is more reasonable than to believe what God says, to trust his promises, and to rely upon his character? What is more reasonable than faith?

CHAPTER V.

PRAYER—PENITENCE—SUBMISSION—A FORGIVING SPIRIT—OBJECTS OF PRAYER—THANKSGIVING AND PRAISE.

IT is our duty to pray to God. We are dependent upon him for life and all things. It is reasonable that the child who is dependent upon his father should ask him for the things he needs. It is reasonable that the child who has disobeyed his father should ask his forgiveness. God has commanded us to pray, and has promised to answer our prayers. "Call unto me and I will answer thee." Jer., xxxiii. 3. "He will regard the prayer of the destitute." Ps. cii. 17. "He heareth the prayer of the righteous." Prov., xv. 29. Christ says, "Ask and ye shall receive, seek and ye shall find, knock and it shall be opened." Matt., vii. 7. "The fervent effectual prayer of a righteous man availeth much." James, v. 16.

We are to pray, believing that we shall be heard, if we "ask according to his will." 1 John, v. 14.

We are not to expect miracles in answer to prayer. A miracle is a direct exercise of the divine power—an act not in accordance with the laws of nature. How God can, in answer to prayer, bring about events without interfering with the laws of nature, we do not know. He declares that he has done so, and will do so. When God says he will do a thing, we must not refuse to believe him, because we do not know how he will do it.

It is objected, that it is unreasonable to suppose that the omnipotent and omniscient Ruler of the Universe can be influenced by the prayer of a weak, ignorant mortal. The question is a question of fact. Has God said that he will hear prayer? If he has said so, all suppositions respecting the reasonableness or unreasonableness of the fact are out of place.

It is objected that the efficacy of prayer is inconsistent with the unchangeableness of God. If prayer causes him to do what he would not otherwise do, it produces a change in him. He is no longer unchangeable.

To this it may be replied, that the unchangeableness of God relates to his character. His character is unchangeable. He always acts on the same holy principles. He does to-day what he did not do yesterday, and will do to-morrow what he does not do to-day; but there is no change in the principles on which he acts. Some seem to confound unchangeableness with inactivity. Rightly viewed, it will be seen that his unchangeableness will not prevent his answering such prayers as are offered according to his will.

It is said, God does not need information as to our wants. He knows all things, and is infinitely wise, and has his plan for conducting the affairs of the universe, and will not turn aside from it to meet the wishes of individuals.

No doubt our Heavenly Father knoweth that we have need of these things. No doubt he is infinitely wise, and acts on an infinitely wise plan ; but it may be a part of that plan to do certain things in answer to prayers offered according to his will. It *is* a part of his plan, for he has said so in his holy word.

The Bible records many examples of the efficacy of prayer. "Elias was a man subject to like passions as we are, and he prayed earnestly that it might not rain ; and it rained not on the earth by the space of three years and six months. And he prayed again, and the heaven gave rain, and the earth brought forth her fruit." James, v. 17.

Many persons in all ages have from their own experience borne testimony to the fact, that God hears and answers prayer.

There have been men who, under the influence of excited feeling, imagined they received answers to prayer, when they did not. This does not weaken the testimony of wise and sober men.

The duty of prayer involves the duty of penitence. Prayer must be accompanied by penitence and confession.

God commands "all men everywhere to repent." Acts, xvii. 30. "Repent ye, and believe the Gospel." Mark, i. 15. Calls to repentance abound in the Scriptures.

It is reasonable that we should repent. We have all sinned, and ought to be sorry for our sins. Repentance is sorrow for sin. True repentance is such a sorrow as makes the subject of it desire to avoid all sin in future. Fear of punishment is not repentance. Remorse of conscience is not repentance. Sorrow for sin for its own sake, and because it was committed against our Heavenly Father, accompanied with a desire to avoid sin altogether, is repentance.

The child has transgressed the commands and injured the feelings of his father. He is sincerely sorry for it, and earnestly desires forgiveness, and fully purposes never to repeat the act of transgression. That child is penitent. When we have similar feelings towards our Heavenly Father, we are penitent.

Penitence is the condition of pardon. "If my people which are called by my name shall humble themselves, and pray, and seek my face, and turn from their wicked ways, then will I hear from heaven, and will forgive their sin, and will heal their land." 2 Chron., vii. 14. "If we confess our sins, he is faithful and just to forgive us our sins." 1 John, i. 9.

Penitence is an appropriate condition of mind for application for pardon. If a man has done wrong, and has no sense of the wrong done, and is not sorry for it, and has no desire to avoid repeating it, there is no propriety in his asking for pardon. Under such circumstances, an application for pardon would rather be an insulting than an humble petition. Penitence does not atone for sin. Penitence does not merit forgiveness; but it is the required and appropriate condition of forgiveness. Forgiveness is an exercise of mercy. Mercy is favor shown to the undeserving.

We must pray with faith, that is, with confidence in God's promise to hear and answer prayer. The prayer of faith is the prayer of one who implicitly trusts the promises of God.

Confidence in God's promises does not require us to believe that every specific petition will be granted. God's promises are conditioned upon our asking in a proper spirit, and for objects that are according to his will. We may ask amiss and not receive, and yet his promise shall hold good.

Some think they must believe that they shall receive the specific thing asked for. They are about to pray for the recovery of a friend who is seriously ill. They endeavor to believe that he will recover; because they regard this belief as the condition of effectual prayer. They do not succeed; for belief does not follow the bidding of the will, that is, we cannot believe a thing by willing to believe it. Belief requires evidence, and where evidence is wanting, there can be no real belief. This error originated in a remark of Christ relative to the faith of miracles.

We must pray with submission. Prayer without the spirit of submission is dictation. The child who is confident that his parent knows better than he does what is for his good, asks in submission to his father's better knowledge. He desires what he asks for, provided his father thinks it is best for him to have it.

This is the attitude of mind with which we should approach God in prayer. He knows what is best for us, and for the interests of truth and righteousness. We should desire nothing which he does not see that it is best for us to have. Christ closed the most earnest prayer, perhaps, that was ever offered on earth, with "not my will, but thine be done." Luke, xxii. 42.

It is our duty to pray with a forgiving spirit. It is unreasonable for one who desires forgiveness for the wrong he has done, to cherish hostility to those who have injured him. Christ illustrates this duty and the reasonableness of it by a striking parable. "Therefore is the kingdom of heaven likened unto a certain king who would take account of his servants. And when he had begun to reckon, one was brought unto him which owed him ten thousand talents. But forasmuch as he had not to pay, his lord commanded him to be sold, and his wife and children and all that he had, and payment to be made. The servant therefore fell down, and worshipped him saying, Lord, have patience with me, and I will pay thee all. Then the Lord of that servant was moved with compassion, and loosed him, and forgave him the debt.

"But the same servant went out and found one of his fellow servants which owed him an hundred pence: and he laid hands on him, and took him by the throat saying, Pay me that thou owest. And his fellow servant fell down at his feet and besought him saying, Have patience with me, and I will pay thee all. And he would not, but went and cast him into prison till he should pay the debt. So when his fellow servants saw what was done, they were very sorry, and came and told their Lord all that was done.

"Then his Lord after that he had called him, said unto him, O thou wicked servant, I forgave thee all that debt, because thou desiredst me. Shouldst not thou also have had compassion on thy fellow servant, even as I had pity on thee? And his lord was wroth, and delivered him to the tormentors, till he should pay all that was due unto him.

"So likewise shall my heavenly Father do also unto you, if ye from your hearts forgive not every one his brother their trespasses." Matt., xviii. 23–35. "But if ye forgive not men their trespasses, neither will your Father forgive your trespasses." Matt., vi. 15.

A forgiving spirit is not inconsistent with a just

regard to our rights of person and property, and the enforcement of the laws of the land.

It is our duty to pray for the pardon of our sins, for wisdom and strength to do the will of God, for the blessing of God upon our enterprises and labors, for the happiness and prosperity of others, and for the extension of God's kingdom. These are the general topics for prayer. The Apostle gives direction that prayer be offered in connection with everything that concerns us. "Be careful for nothing; but in everything by prayer and supplication with thanksgiving let your requests be made known unto God." Phil., iv. 6.

It is our duty to pray for the influence and aid of the Holy Spirit. Our moral powers are weakened by reason of sin. We need an influence from without to give us aspirations for excellence and to aid us in using the means for acquiring it. The Scriptures clearly teach that a divine influence is exerted upon the mind, leading it towards perfection. How this influence can be exerted without interfering with man's freedom as a moral agent, we do not know. We know the fact on the testimony of God. This influence is commonly exerted in connection with the truth. The mind is enabled to see the truth more clearly, and is rendered more susceptible to the impression it is adapted to make.

The Holy Spirit is represented as a teacher, comforter, inspirer of love to God and of prayer, and sanctifier of the soul. The gift of the Spirit thus includes the greatest of blessings. This gift is promised to those who desire it. "If ye, being evil, know how to give good gifts to your children, how much more shall your heavenly Father give the Holy Spirit to them that ask him." Luke, xi. 13.

It is our duty to render to God thanksgiving. That it is our duty to be grateful for benefits received is a self-evident truth. Thanksgiving is the appropriate expression of our gratitude. The Scriptures insist on this duty. "Offer unto God thanksgiving." Ps. l. 14. "Giving thanks always for all things unto God and the Father, in the name of our Lord Jesus Christ." Eph., v. 20.

Connected with thanksgiving is praise. Injunctions to praise abound in the Scriptures. "Sing unto the Lord with thanksgiving." Ps. cxlvii. 7. "Speaking to yourselves in psalms and hymns, and spiritual songs, singing and making melody in your heart to the Lord." Eph., v. 19. Praise is represented as one of the employments of heaven.

Does not the duty of singing praise to God involve the duty of learning to sing, just as the duty of studying God's word involves the duty of learning to read? Should not vocal music as well as reading be taught in our schools?

CHAPTER VI.

STUDY OF THE BIBLE—ADVANTAGES.

It is our duty to study the word of God. This duty is involved in that of studying the character of God. It is, indeed, involved in all the duties that have been mentioned. Still, its importance is so great that it is proper to give it separate consideration.

God has written a book for our benefit. Hence it is our duty to study it, and to seek to derive from it all the benefit it was intended to convey.

The Bible gives us knowledge of infinite value, which could be obtained from no other source. It makes known to us truths concerning God, which we could never learn from nature, nor from the highest exercise of reason. Nature teaches us that God is infinitely wise and powerful, but is he infinitely just? The mere suspicion of injustice on the part of God, would throw a pall of darkness over the universe. But nature cannot assure us that God is just.

In order that we may infer, from a man's actions, that he is perfectly just, all his actions must be conformed to the law of justice. If some of his actions are just and some of them unjust, we cannot infer that he is a perfectly just man. If some of his actions *appear* to be unjust, we cannot be certain that he is a perfectly just man.

In like manner, all the indications in nature in regard to the justice of God must point in one direction, or we cannot conclude from them that God is perfectly just.

Now what are the indications? They are twofold. There are many examples, in the works of Providence, of the wicked punished and the righteous rewarded. These indicate justice on the part of God. But there are many examples of an opposite character. The wicked are often prosperous even to the close of life. The righteous are often oppressed and afflicted all their days. These facts do not indicate justice on the part of the Governor of the world. If we were left to the light of nature, we could come to no certain conclusion in regard to the justice of God. But the Bible removes the difficulty. It reveals a future world of retribution in which all men shall be rewarded according to the deeds done in the body. It assures us that God is perfectly just.

In like manner, the indications of nature in regard to the benevolence of God are, taken as a whole, equivocal. Benevolence tends to produce happiness. Some of the arrangements of nature tend to promote happiness, and some tend to promote misery. There are the sunshine, the delightful breeze, and the refreshing shower. There are also the storm, the pestilence, and the earthquake. From some of these indications, we should infer benevolence on the part of their author. From others, we should infer malignity. We need light from above to enable us to reconcile all the indications of nature with the benevolence of God. This light the Bible furnishes. It shows us that all suffering is the consequence of sin, —the result of a system of justice to be perfected hereafter. It assures us of the infinite benevolence of God.

Nature can give us no assurance that pardon can be had on repentance. The truth that pardon can be had, every member of the human family is interested in knowing. Every one knows that he is a sinner. Every one knows that he needs forgiveness; but the Bible alone informs him how it may be obtained.

In nature there are some indications which suggest the possibility of severing the connection between the violation of God's law and the penalty attached to the violation. The transgressor of the laws of health, if he reforms and takes remedies in season, may recover from the effect of his transgressions. This suggests that the transgressor of the moral law, may by timely repentance and reformation escape the penalty. There are other violations of physical law, which are invariably followed by their penalties. Sever the jugular vein and death is certain. No acts of repentance can, in such cases avert the penalty. May not the same be true of violations of the moral law? There are some indications in nature which suggest the possibility of pardon,—there are more which point in the direction of inflexible justice.

We need therefore the light of revelation to teach that God is merciful and gracious, forgiving iniquity, transgression and sins,—that sinners can be forgiven for Christ's sake. "Even as God for Christ's sake hath forgiven you." Eph., iv. 32. "In whom we have redemption through his blood, the forgiveness of sin." Eph., i. 7.

Hence the Bible should be studied, because it teaches truths of infinite value which cannot be gained from any other source.

The Bible should be studied, because it has a tendency to develop and purify all our powers. It is a mistake to suppose that it tends to improve our moral powers only. It has a tendency to improve our intellectual, and social, as well as our moral nature.

All our powers are improved by exercise. The Bible has a tendency to exercise all our powers, and hence, to improve them.

The Bible contains a system of truth, just as nature contains a system of truth. It requires careful study to discover it, and that study improves the mind.

The facts from which the science of astronomy is derived appear, at first view, to have very little connection with each other. It took centuries of observation before the system which underlies those facts and shows that they belong to one harmonious whole, was discovered.

The facts of the Bible from which the science of theology is derived, seem at first view to have but little connection. They lie scattered as it were throughout the Bible. There are facts of history and biography, proverbial maxims, songs of praise, prophecies, and precepts. When carefully studied, a connected system is evolved, and all the various facts of the Bible are found to be parts of one harmonious whole. The study of systematic truth, especially when that truth relates to the highest and most important themes with which the mind can hold converse, must be improving to the mind.

Again, the mind is improved by coming in contact with minds of power. The books which it is most profitable to read are not those which convey the largest amount of information, but those that are instinct with power. In reading the work of a superior mind, the mind of the reader comes in contact with the mind of the writer and receives a portion of his power.

Now in studying the Bible, the mind comes in contact with the divine mind. If to bring the mind in contact with a powerful human mind be productive of benefit, much more must it be so to bring it in contact with the divine mind! If the benefit of communion with a human mind be in proportion to the power of that mind, how great must be the benefit of communing with the infinite mind!

The object of revelation is to restore the soul to its original perfection. A well developed intellect is necessary to a perfect soul. Hence the Bible is, as we have seen, adapted to develop the intellect. It is also adapted to develop taste, or the power of perceiving and enjoying beauty. There are, in the Bible, many passages of unequalled beauty and sublimity.

It is also adapted to exercise the imagination. Witness the imagery of some of the Hebrew prophets, and especially that of Saint John in the Revelation.

It is also adapted to exalt and purify our affections. It makes the exercise of love pervade all our duties. It sets before our affections an object of perfect loveliness in the character of our Heavenly Father. In short, it is perfectly adapted to form wisdom, strength and beauty of character,—to render us perfect men in Christ Jesus. It is therefore infinitely more worthy of study than any other volume.

The Bible should be *studied,* not kept as a talisman, nor formally read as a mechanical exercise. It should be studied with reverence, but the same rules of interpretation should be applied to it as to other books. We are to search the Scriptures. To honest and vigorous exercise of mind, there should be added prayer for divine illumination. "Open thou mine eyes that I may behold wondrous things out of thy law." Ps. cxix. 18.

In studying the Bible it is important to notice the relation between its doctrines and its precepts. Some endeavor to separate them, when, in truth, they are inseparable. Some regard the precepts as having a closer relation to practice, and hence as more important. They do not regard the doctrines of the Bible as having any relation to practice.

The doctrines of the Bible are to its precepts, what the principles of arithmetic are to its practical rules. The doctrines are the principles whence the precepts are drawn. We need to understand the doctrines in order to understand the reasons of the precepts.

The study of the Bible should be accompanied with devout meditation. To know what the Bible teaches is one thing : to have its truths influential in directing our actions and moulding our characters is another thing. That truths may be thus influential, the attention of the mind must be long and steadily directed to them.

CHAPTER VII.

CULTURE AND CARE OF THE BODY—LAWFUL RELAXATIONS—SELF-DEFENCE.

God made man for a certain end. It is man's duty not to defeat that end. He should endeavor to be what God made him to be. God made him to be a man. He has therefore no right to be a brute. It is his duty to be a man. It is his duty to do everything in his power to realize the idea of a perfect manhood.

Man is composed of body and mind. They are mysteriously united and exert a reciprocal influence on each other. A feeble and diseased body often enfeebles the action of the mind. A disordered mind often produces bodily disease. Both must be in a healthful condition, both must be properly developed in order to a perfect mind.

A well developed body is of more consequence than is commonly supposed. The body is the instrument of the mind. If the instrument is out of order, the skill of the agent may be lost. This shows that those are in error who think it a duty to cultivate the mind, but regard the culture of the body as optional.

It is our duty to become acquainted with the structure of our bodies, because this knowledge is necessary to an intelligent care of them. Intimately connected with a knowledge of the structure of our bodies, is a knowledge of the laws of health, that is, the rules we should follow in order to avoid disease.

Our bodily powers are developed by exercise. Activity and industry are necessary to the healthful growth of our bodies,—necessary to the development of bodily strength. Hence habits of inactivity and idleness are wrong.

Activity must not be continued to the point of hurtful exhaustion. Excessive industry is wrong; for it uses up the staple of life before the time.

It is our duty to avoid all intemperance in eating and drinking. Gluttony as well as drunkenness is a vice, and a debasing one. God has rendered eating and drinking pleasant, but the pleasures thus occasioned are incidental to the nourishment of the body. We were made to eat that our bodies may be nourished, not for the sake of the pleasure of eating. The epicure makes that an end which was designed to be incidental to the pursuit of a higher end.

All excess in eating and drinking tends to injure the health and enfeeble the mind. All injurious articles of food and drink should be avoided. Duty requires the moderate use of useful and lawful things, and entire abstinence from hurtful and unlawful things.

No one has a right wilfully or through carelessness to injure his health. Health is necessary to a discharge of the duties of life. We have no right to incapacitate ourselves for performing the duties of life. We have no right to render ourselves unable to pay our debts by casting our money into the fire. No one has a right to say, "my body is my own and I can neglect or abuse it if I choose to do so."

It is our duty to avoid such amusements as are injurious to health and morals. It is lawful to take relaxation and enjoy amusements. The bow is not always to be bent. The human mind cannot long endure continued vigorous exertion. There are legitimate amusements. There are legitimate social enjoyments. God has made us social beings. The perfect example of Christ authorizes us to be present at the marriage gathering and at the hospitable board. But lawful amusements and enjoyments may be indulged in to excess. In regard to these things, the voice of reason and of revelation unite in saying to every one, "Do thyself no harm." God prohibits those things only which are injurious to ourselves or to others.

It is our duty to avoid all unnecessary exposure whereby our health may be impaired, and, when it is impaired, to use the remedies best adapted to restore it. Hence it is our duty to have recourse to the prescriptions of men of science and skill, and not to those of quacks and imposters.

If it is our duty to take care of our health, much more is it our duty to take care of our lives. We have no right to do anything that shall needlessly put our lives in peril.

It is our duty to defend ourselves against lawless violence. Christ did not teach the doctrine of non-resistance. When he said, "If any man smite you on one cheek, turn the other also," he did not intend to teach a doctrine which gives impunity to violence. He did not mean to forbid self-defence, or an appeal to the protection of the laws. He meant to inculcate a forbearing spirit, and to forbid a retaliatory spirit. To forbid self-defence when the emergency requires it, and to forbid efforts to bring the violators of law to just punishment, would be to give society over to the wicked—would be to authorize anarchy. No one can believe that Christ intended to teach such doctrines.

That we have a right to defend ourselves from lawless violence, when an appeal cannot be made to the protection of the law, is a self-evident truth. We instinctively exercise self-defence, and conscience approves the act, that is, we see that it is right.

This principle does not authorize us to resent and punish every insult, or to punish such personal wrongs as can be referred to a legal tribunal. Government is for the punishment of evil doers, and to it should they be handed over, except when the emergency requires instant defence.

It is sometimes our duty to suffer wrong, without even appealing to the laws for redress. Christ's example teaches us that we are sometimes silently to suffer wrong, and to "commit our cause to Him who judgeth righteously." But if a lawless attempt is made to take our life, it is our duty to defend it, even at the expense of the life of our assailant. In such a case, the right and duty of self-defence would be clear.

CHAPTER VIII.

DISCIPLINE AND DEVELOPMENT OF MIND—SELF-CONTROL—ANGER.

It is our duty to develop and discipline our minds, so that they may be efficient instruments for performing the work given us to do. Every one sees that it would not be right for us to dwarf our bodies or paralyze our limbs, so that they would be unfit to perform their functions. On the same principle, it would be wrong for us to dwarf our minds, thus unfitting them for accomplishing what they might otherwise accomplish. Mental power is far more important and valuable than bodily power. It is a much greater wrong to allow it to run to waste.

Our mental, like our bodily powers, are developed by exercise. The object of education is not so much to acquire knowledge as to develop power. One may have a great deal of knowledge and very little power. Of course, he can do but little. Knowledge is power only as it prompts to exertion, and gives a right direction to it.

No one can develop and discipline the mind of another. He can tell him how to do it, but each one must do the work for himself. Every one must educate himself, if he is educated at all.

The degree of culture which each one is under obligation to bestow upon his mind, must be determined by the circumstances in which he is placed.

It is our duty to train our minds to perceive truth clearly. Man was made to act wisely. A knowledge of the truth is necessary to wise action. Action from false principles cannot be wise action. A man who goes into the manufacture of gunpowder on erroneous chemical principles, or rather in ignorance of the true chemical principles which underlie the art, will be almost certain to fail. If he succeeds, his success will be accidental. In like manner, he who enters upon any department of effort, in ignorance of the facts and principles concerned, cannot pursue a wise and efficient course.

It is our duty to train our minds to an accurate perception of truth in relation to duty. Our great, in truth, our sole business here is to do duty. We must know our duty in order to do it. Ignorance of duty will not excuse us from doing it, unless that ignorance be invincible.

It is our duty to acquire accurate knowledge, so far as it is possible, in regard to all subjects, in relation to which we are called to act. Where positive knowledge cannot be acquired, it is our duty to form as accurate opinions as possible. Our action in relation to a given subject will, if we act as rational beings, be determined by our knowledge or opinions in relation to that subject. Hence, if we are responsible for our actions, we are responsible for the opinions that determine the character of our actions.

Our powers were given us for action—for wise action. Action can be wise only as it is in accordance with truth. If a man undertakes to be an agriculturist, his labor will be effective only as it is put forth in accordance with those rules and principles which experience has shown to be true. He has no right to waste labor by doing that which will bring about no valuable end. It is duty to acquire the knowledge necessary to render his labor productive.

Suppose it to be one's duty to visit with dispatch and economy certain cities in Europe. It would be his duty to acquaint himself with the relative position of said cities, and of the best modes of conveyance. If in any case accurate knowledge cannot be acquired, he must do his best to form as accurate an opinion as possible. For example, if there are two lines of travel, each claiming certain advantages, he may not be able to learn which is absolutely the best. In view of the conflicting claims, he may be able to form an opinion as to which is best—he may not be able to acquire actual knowledge. It is his duty to form as accurate an opinion as possible, since his opinion must determine his action.

It is the statesman's duty to promote the best interests of his country. In order that he may frame wise measures, he must have an accurate knowledge of the condition and wants of the country. So far as his knowledge is inadequate, his action is liable to be unwise. If it be wise, it will be wise only by accident.

In many cases, his conduct must be determined by his opinions. That those opinions should, as far as possible, be correct, is too plain to require argument.

It thus appears that in every sphere of action, men are under obligation to acquire accurate knowledge and form accurate opinions.

The only exception that has been claimed relates to the acquisition of religious knowledge and the formation of religious opinions. On this subject many unsound assertions have been made. It has been affirmed that men are not responsible for their religious belief, and that a correct belief is a matter of no consequence. It is sometimes said that it is no matter what a man's belief is, if his practice be right. This implies that there is no connection between belief and practice, whereas we have seen that, if we act rationally, our action will be as our belief.

A moment's reflection will show that there is the same connection between knowledge and action, in relation to religion, as there is in relation to other objects. We cannot do our duty to God unless we know that God exists, and that he sustains certain relations to us. If we have inaccurate ideas of God, we must of necessity have inaccurate ideas of duty towards him. We cannot know our duties in relation to Christ's mission, unless we have accurate knowledge of the nature of that mission.

The Bible is the source of a large amount of positive knowledge. There are some things so clearly revealed that we may be said *to know* them. There are statements in the Bible, the meaning of which are not perfectly clear to us. In regard to these, we have beliefs rather than knowledge. Those beliefs are often as influential, and necessarily so, as our knowledge. Hence it is important that they should be correct. Hence it is our duty to use all the means in our power to form correct beliefs. If through carelessness in the examination of evidence, or through the influence of prejudice, we form erroneous opinions, and are thus led to perform wrong actions, we are responsible both for the actions and the opinions. We were made to do right.

It may be asked, suppose a man is perfectly sincere in his erroneous belief, and acts in accordance with it, will not his action be accepted as right?

Consider the matter in the light of analogy. Suppose a man owes A a sum of money. He meets B, and mistakes him for A., and hands him the money. He designs to pay his just debts. He designs to do right. Has he discharged his obligation to his creditor? Will A accept his sincerity in lieu of the money due him?

Suppose a man sincerely believes it to be his duty to worship an idol, will God, on account of his sincerity in error, acccept that worship in lieu of the worship due to himself?

His sincerity would lessen his guilt, but would not remove it altogether—would not change wrong into right. To worship an idol, knowing it to be his duty to worship God, would indeed be a far greater sin, than to worship an idol under the belief that he was doing right.

Correct religious knowledge is, therefore, important, as the directory of religious duty. Correct knowledge without reference to practice is of no value.

It is our duty to deliver our minds from the power of prejudice. Prejudice interferes with the accurate perception of truth. If we have a prejudice in favor of a proposition, we receive it as a truth on a very small amount of evidence. If we have a prejudice against a person, we readily believe a statement to his disadvantage. The only department of truth, free from the influence of prejudice, is mathematical truth.

To free our minds from the influence of every kind of prejudice is a difficult task. It must be done, or we cannot have accurate perceptions of truth and duty.

It is our duty to train our minds to perceive and enjoy beauty. God has given us power to perceive and enjoy beauty, and has scattered beauty profusely throughout his works. To turn away from it with indifference is to treat him with disrespect.

The useful must ever claim the larger share of our attention, but the beautiful must not be neglected. Beauty has its utilities. It is a source of pure and elevated enjoyment. What are usually termed the pleasures of taste,—the pleasures resulting from a perception of the beauties of nature and of the fine arts, are refining and elevating in their influence. They are higher than the pleasures of sense, and inferior only to those resulting from the exercise of our best affections on their proper objects.

The love of beauty is not the love of holiness and must not be mistaken for it. The worship of beauty must not be substituted for the worship of God.

True religion has a tendency to form a beautiful character, and so far as it fails to do so, the failure must be owing to the want of a right application of its principles.

It is our duty to control and subjugate our tempers. The excitement of passion renders clear perception and sound judgment impossible. The angry man sees everything through a distorted medium. He thinks he acts perfectly reasonable in all that he does under the promptings of his passion. When his passion has subsided, he sees his folly. Anger interferes with the performance of all our duties. The apostle commands us to "lay aside all anger," and not to let the "sun go down upon your wrath."

He who cannot control himself, can never have any considerable degree of control over others. So far as a man is unable to control his temper, he loses the respect of his fellow men. "He that is slow to anger is better than the mighty; and he that ruleth his spirit, than he that taketh a city." Prov., xvi. 32.

Men differ greatly in their natural tempers. Some are calm and not easily moved, others are very susceptible of angry feeling. It is difficult for such to get perfect control of their tempers, but it can be done. It will require time and effort, but it can be done.

We can control our tempers by constantly trying to do it. The reason why some persons have no control over their tempers will be found in the fact that they do not try to have any control. They do not try to restrain themselves. Occasionally, when in the presence of strangers, perhaps, they may put some restraint upon themselves; but ordinarily, they yield to every impulse of passion.

We may not be able to prevent the rising of temper, but we can avoid giving any expression to it. When anger prompts us to utter harsh words, we can keep our lips firmly closed. If we habitually refuse to give expression to a feeling, by word or deed, its strength will continually decay.

It may be asked, is it ever right to be angry? The Bible says, "Be ye angry and sin not." Eph., iv. 26. This would indicate that there is a kind of anger that is not sinful. God is said to be angry with the wicked. By this is meant his holy disapprobation of sin—his righteous indignation at wrong-doing. We are so made, that we cannot help feeling indignation when we witness acts of injustice and cruelty. This feeling is right.

Anger in its ordinary meaning is the perversion of that capacity of our nature that leads us to look with disapprobation and indignation at wrong-doing.

The duty of self-control has respect to other feelings as well as anger. Our appetites are to be under our control. They were given us for certain purposes. They are to be kept within the limits they were designed to occupy. Within those limits they are sources of lawful enjoyment. Paul said, "I keep my body under and keep it in subjection."

All our passions should be under the control of reason and conscience, that is, they should be exercised only when it is reasonable and right for them to be exercised. Just in proportion as a man is under the dominion of his passions, he approximates to the brute creation.

CHAPTER IX.

REGULATION OF OUR DESIRES.

OUR desires are the immediate causes of our actions. We never act unless we have a desire to do so. We may do that, which, in itself considered, we do not desire to do. The cause of our doing it may be a desire to avoid the consequences of not doing it. A child may not desire to go to school; yet he goes, being led to do so by a desire to avoid the punishment that would follow his failure to go.

Our desires being thus the causes of our actions, the regulation of them becomes a very important duty.

Some desires are original and some acquired. Our original desires are those which are the result of our creation—which were implanted in our nature by God. These are possessed, though in different degrees of strength, by all men. The desire of knowledge, of society, of property, of esteem, are original desires. All our original desires are right when properly exercised. Whatever belongs to our nature as it came from the hand of God, is right.

There are desires which are not common to all

men. They are acquired by some men. The desires for tobacco and alcoholic drinks, are acquired desires. Some acquired desires are right and others wrong.

Our original desires may be perverted and directed towards wrong objects, and lead us to adopt wrong means for their gratification : in such cases they become wrong.

It is our duty to cherish the desire for knowledge. The fact that this desire is given us, in connection with the capacity for knowing, shows that it ought to be gratified. "That the soul be without knowledge is not good." Prov., xix. 2.

This desire can be gratified by turning our attention to objects of knowledge.

We should not allow this desire to lead us to attempt to know that which is beyond our powers. Our powers are limited. There are some things which we can know : there are some things which beings with higher powers can know, which we cannot know.

We should seek to acquire useful knowledge. We are not to indulge an idle curiosity—a desire to know things that are in no way useful. Some spend their whole lives in laborious trifling—searching for knowledge which, when found, is of no use to them or to others.

Useful knowledge is not confined to facts capable of application to the ordinary pursuits of life. Whatever tends to expand, elevate, strengthen, and purify the soul is useful.

There are knowledges which are injurious and debasing. These should be carefully avoided. We cannot willingly increase our knowledge of evil without guilt.

The desire for society is natural to man. Scarcely any punishment, short of death, is more severe than that of separating one entirely from the society of his fellow men.

This desire should not lead us to associate with men simply to avoid solitude, or to pass away the time. We should seek the society of those whose influence will be beneficial. Our social nature was given us that we might associate with the good—not with the evil.

We are not to separate ourselves from the wicked, on the pharisaic principle, Stand by, I am holier than thou. We are to follow Christ's example, by mingling with all classes of men, for the purpose of doing them good. But when we would indulge the desire for society, we should select as our companions "the excellent of the earth."

The desire of property is natural to man. God designed that men should produce and possess property, and hence implanted the desire of possession. Property, wealth, is necessary to the comfort of man, and is a necessary condition of civilization. The leisure and means of mental and social improvement cannot be had, unless there is in the community a certain amount of wealth.

It is lawful to gratify this desire by the use of just and honorable means. Whenever it seeks gratification by unjust and dishonorable means, it has become perverted and wrong. When excessive, it leads to avarice, one of the meanest of vices.

This desire must be subordinate to the desire of pleasing God and doing his will. "Seek ye first the kingdom of God and his righteousness." Matt., vi. 33.

It may be asked, to what extent may this desire be indulged? How long may a man continue to accumulate property?

So long as he conducts his operations wisely, and with strict integrity. So long as he pursues such a course, he will benefit others by his operations, and he may benefit himself so long as in so doing he benefits others.

The desire of esteem is natural to man. A man must become very much debased before he can lose all desire of esteem on the part of his fellow men. It is doubtful whether this desire is ever wholly eradicated.

It is right to seek the esteem of men by right means. It is right to seek it by rendering ourselves worthy of esteem. It is not right to seek it in any other way.

This desire often becomes excessive. In many, the desire for popularity is so strong, that truth and honor are sacrificed in its pursuit. The question such men ask is not, What is right? but, What will secure popularity? That which they think will please men, is substituted for that which will please God. "For they loved the praise of men more than the praise of God." John, xii. 43.

The desire of excellence is a natural desire. Its direct tendency, when properly directed, is to our improvement. It leads to emulation, but emulation is not necessarily evil. Paul appealed to this principle, when he was making pecuniary collections for the members of the church at Jerusalem.

The desire of distinction is closely allied to the desire of excellence. It is lawful to seek for distinction by the use of honorable means.

The apostle commends those "who by patient continuance in well-doing seek for glory, and honor, and immortality." Rom., ii. 7.

The love of distinction must not be a ruling motive. It must be subordinate to the desire to do, in all things, the will of God.

The desire of distinction, when not rightly regulated, leads to jealousy and envy. When the soul is under the dominion of jealousy and envy, all the nobler feelings decay. No evil passion is more painful to the person who exercises it, and more blighting in its effects upon the character.

There is more envy in the hearts of men than they are willing to admit. Much of the criticism of character which we hear is owing to envy, though it assumes the garb of justice.

To guard against it, we should be careful to exercise an exact, if not generous justice towards those who are liable to become to us objects of envy. If it give us uneasiness to hear one praised, let us take heed lest this vile passion find a lodgment in our bosoms.

The desire of power is a natural desire. If indulged for selfish purposes it is wrong. It is not lawful to desire power for its own sake, or as an end. We are commanded to be strong in the Lord—strong to do the work he would have us do.

The possession of power is a dangerous trust, and one liable to be abused. Few have possessed power over their fellow men without abusing it.

The legitimate desire of power may degenerate into ambition. The question may be asked, is ambition right? Is it lawful to cherish an ambitious spirit? The answer depends upon the definition given to the term ambition. Some speak of a holy ambition, but it is doubtful whether that is a proper form of expression. Ambition, as commonly understood, implies such a desire of advancement as may lead to the use of improper measures for its attainment.

The desire for happiness is an original desire. There is, therefore, a lawful sphere for its gratification.

Happiness is not something external to the soul like wealth. It is a condition of the soul. The question arises, how can this condition be secured? The answer must be derived from experience, and the teachings of God.

God made us to be happy, or he would not have given us this desire. It is therefore our duty to be happy. But we must be happy in the way designed by him. We must not say "God made us to be happy; the gratification of our desires yields happiness, therefore we are to gratify our desires." Some of our desires are to be gratified and some are to be repressed. We must make a distinction.

It is a general fact or law of our nature that the gratification of desire is pleasant. The gratification of the desire for food or the desire for property is pleasant. So also the gratification of revenge, or the desire to injure one is pleasant. The gratification of our evil passions is pleasant for the time being. It cannot therefore be right for us to seek for happiness in the gratification of all our desires.

Virtuous desires are in themselves pleasant, and pleasant in their gratification. Vicious desires are in themselves painful, yet in their gratification pleasant.

The soul as it came from the hand of the Creator had no evil desires. The general law, that the gratification of desire is attended with pleasure, was therefore an appropriate law. Now when evil desires spring up in the soul, God does not repeal the original law with respect to the gratification of desire; but he shows that he approves virtue and disapproves vice, by making the exercise of virtuous desires pleasant, and the exercise of vicious desires painful: and while the gratification of a vicious desire is followed by a momentary enjoyment, it is also followed by lasting pain. One feels hatred toward his neighbor and does him an injury. There is a momentary enjoyment connected with the gratification of his evil desire, but it is followed by a sense of guilt and remorse, which will be felt, at intervals at least, till the guilt be removed.

Happiness is the result of the proper exercise of all our powers. It may be said that there is enjoyment in rest, bodily and mental. True, but rest presupposes exertion, and the rest yielding the highest happiness derivable from rest, is the rest following the proper exercise of our powers.

There is enjoyment resulting from the proper exercise of our physical powers. There is a higher enjoyment resulting from the exercise of our intellectual and esthetic powers. There is still higher enjoyment resulting from the exercise of our affections. Now as it is God's will that all our powers should be properly exercised, happiness will be secured by doing his will. He who loves God with all his heart and his neighbor as himself, is a happy man. He will be led so to exercise his powers as to secure the greatest amount of happiness attainable by man. God's will is a directory for the attainment of happiness. Human happiness is the incidental result of making the performance of God's will, the object of life.

CHAPTER X.

DUTIES OF THE FAMILY CIRCLE.

It is our duty to cultivate the affections which unite us with our fellow men. We are endowed with various affections, that is, we are capable of exercising different kinds and degrees of love towards those sustaining certain relations to us. It is of course our duty to develop and exercise these affections according to the design of him who made them a part of our nature.

It is our duty to love, reverence, and obey our parents. We were the objects of parental love and care, before our powers were sufficiently developed to be aware of it. The tenderness and care that watched over our infancy, and ministered to the wants of later years, call for love and gratitude in return. Thus the duty of blended love and gratitude springs from the relation we sustain to our parents, and from benefits bestowed by them.

Love to parents is natural, spontaneous, but still it requires cultivation. It may be cultivated by reflecting on the parental relation, and on the kindness received, and by reference to the authority of God.

God has rendered us, in early life, entirely dependent upon our parents, and subject to their control. His commandment is "Honor thy father and thy mother." Ex., xx. 12. And "Children, obey your parents in the Lord, for this is right." Eph., vi. 1. Hence we are under obligation always to treat our parents with marked respect and to obey them "in all things," that is in all things that are according to the will of God. The authority of God is higher than the authority of the parent. If the commands of a parent come in conflict with the commands of God, "we ought to obey God rather than men."

When the child becomes of age, he is no longer under the authoritative control of the parent, but his obligation to love and honor him remains. If the parent is in want of assistance, it is the duty of the child to furnish that assistance, if it be within his power. Gratitude for benefits received requires it. God wills that children "roquite their parents." 1 Tim., v. 4. When the feebleness of old age arrives, parents should receive from children the tenderness and care which they themselves received in infancy and childhood.

The affection of a child for his parent is of necessity modified by the character and conduct of the parent. A kind and loving parent receives more love than a harsh and unfeeling one. Some parents are more worthy of their children's love than others. However unworthy a parent may become, so long as the parental relation remains, there are duties springing from that relation, and from those duties the child is not absolved. The conduct of the parent may cancel all obligations to gratitude, but some other obligations will remain.

It is the duty of brothers and sisters to cherish an affectionate regard for each other, and to labor to promote each other's improvement and happiness. The intimate relations in which they are placed in the same family, and commonly beneath the same roof, render love a necessary condition of peace and harmony, without which the object of God in constituting the family would be defeated.

Affection depends, in a measure at least, for its continuance upon courtesy. As it is the duty of members of the same family to love one another, it follows that it is their duty to treat one another with courtesy. Constant familiarity has a tendency to cause a neglect of those forms of politeness, which are intimately connected with the continuance of affection and growth in refinement. The forms of affection as well as of liberty, are essential to the reality.

All tendency to envy, jealousy, and suspicion should be carefully guarded against by all the members of the family circle. In that circle the law of love should be the supreme law. Then will the family be what it was designed to be by its author, one of the most beautiful objects on earth, and a nursery for heaven.

It is the duty of parents to love, cherish, and provide for the wants and the education of their children. Parents feel an instinctive affection for their offspring. This feeling was given by God to secure adequate care for children in the helplessness of infancy. He has made it the duty of parents to care for their children ; but to the obligations of duty he has added the prompting of instinctive and strong affection. It is their duty to strengthen and purify this affection. This may be done by faithfully doing that which affection, regulated by reason, would prompt, by reflecting upon the condition and destiny of the child, and by striving to perform all the parental duties required by God.

It is the duty of the parent to provide for the physical wants of the child. The continuance of its life depends upon the care of the parent. To every parent to whom God gives a child, he says, by his providence, as Pharaoh's daughter said to the Hebrew mother, "Take this child away, and nurse it for me, and I will give thee thy wages." Ex., ii. 9.

It is the duty of the parent to educate his children in the knowledge of God and of duty. This is incumbent upon all parents. All parents are bound to bring up their children "in the nurture and admonition of the Lord." Eph. vi. 4.

It is the duty of parents to teach by example as well as precept. Parental example is always more powerful than parental precept. The best instructions are often neutralized by defective examples.

It is the duty of parents to provide for the intellectual and social education of their children. To what extent this culture must be carried is to be determined by the circumstances of the parent and the capacity of the child. It cannot be the duty of the day-laborer to do as much for the education of his children as the merchant of large means. It cannot be a duty to furnish to one of very limited capacity the advantages which can be useful to those only of superior natural powers.

It is the duty of parents to strive to make home pleasant to their children. Children seldom fall into irregular and vicious habits when they have a happy home. Parents should not allow the cares of life to render them silent, and perhaps morose, at home. They must not only love and labor for their children; they must sympathize with them. The great want of the young heart is sympathy. To their parents, above all others, have they a right to look for sympathy. If they do not find it at home, they will seek for it abroad.

It is the duty of parents to shield their children

as much as possible from evil influences. They should not, for the sake of worldly advantages, place them where they will meet with influences unfavorable to the formation of a virtuous and manly character. All are commanded to pray, "Lead us not into temptation;" hence it is the duty of all to avoid unnecessary temptation, and to avoid leading others into temptation. Especially is this the duty of parents with respect to their children.

The affection which leads to the formation of the marriage relation is the highest form of human affection. The relation that it introduces is the most intimate of earthly relations. "For this cause shall a man leave father and mother, and shall cleave to his wife: and they twain shall be one flesh. Wherefore they are no more twain but one flesh. What therefore God hath joined together, let not man put asunder." Matt., xix. 5.

It is the duty of the husband to love his wife with paramount affection, and to make her happiness his first care. It is the duty of the wife to reciprocate his affection, and to acknowledge him as her head. Eph. v. 23.

The relation of husband and wife is entered into for life, and it cannot be sooner ended without the incurring of guilt by at least one of the parties. The New Testament authorizes divorce for one cause only. Matt., v. 32. Laws which authorize it for other causes, are not in accordance with the law of Christ.

The affection nearest allied to those which exists in the family circle, is that of friendship. God has given us a capacity for friendship and has furnished examples of it in his word. It is a blessed capacity, one that may add greatly to the joys and lessen the sorrows of life.

It is our duty to select our friends wisely, since they will of necessity exert a strong influence over us. We should cherish for them an unselfish affection; for friendship is true only so far as it is disinterested. We should be faithful to their interest in subordination to the will of God. The highest acts of friendship are those tending to render the character of one's friend more perfect. It is related of Jonathan, in the most beautiful instance of friendship ever put on record, that he "went to David into the wood and strengthened his hand in God." 1 Sam., xxiii. 16. To promote one's spiritual perfection is the highest act of friendship.

CHAPTER XI.

DUTIES OF BENEVOLENCE.

It is our duty to exercise benevolence towards our fellow men—towards all men. We are to "do good to all men as we have opportunity." Gal., vi. 10. To this end, we should cultivate a benevolent spirit, in opposition to a selfish spirit. All are liable to become selfish. Self-love, or the natural desire for happiness easily degenerates into selfishness. We must be constantly on our guard lest an undue regard to our own interest lead us to neglect the duties of benevolence.

We should cherish sympathy for those who suffer. This is done by turning our attention to objects adapted to awaken sympathy. We cannot excite our sympathies by an act of will. We can excite them by considering cases of suffering. We can turn aside from such instances, if we choose to do so.

One reason why there is so little apparent feeling for those who are in distress is, that attention is not fixed upon cases of distress. Men are deeply interested in their own pursuits, and do not feel for others, because they do not think of them. Hence it is our duty to seek out those who are in distress. We are not to wait till the objects requiring sympathy force themselves upon our attention. We are to seek them out. Sorrow should have an attraction for us, as it had for Christ.

Our sympathies must be carried out in action. We should not content ourselves with feeling compassion for those who suffer; we must relieve them so far as it lies in our power. True sympathy followed by wise action is true benevolence.

We should also cherish an interest in the welfare of those who are not in distress. They are the children of our common Father, and hence we should not feel indifferent to them. Benevolence would lead us to desire the happiness of all. We should desire and endeavor to exert a good influence on all with whom we come in contact.

Our first duties are towards those with whom we are most intimately connected. But we are under obligation to do good to our neighbors as well as to our relatives. Christ defines our neighbors to be those who need the aid we are able to bestow. Disinterested benevolence, though not the sum of all duty, is nevertheless a very important duty.

It is our duty to give alms to the poor. This is plain from the structure of our nature and the command of God.

Indiscriminate almsgiving is not a duty. "Give to every man that asketh of thee," Luke, vi. 30, is not to be understood literally. Men are not to be supported in idleness and vice. It is our duty to give to the poor, not to impostors. We are not at liberty to give to the wily impostor that which should be given to the necessitous poor. Careful discrimination should be exercised.

The apostle declares that if a man will not work neither shall he eat. Those who by their industry can supply their wants, have no claims upon our charity. When there is any capacity for labor, relief should, if possible, be given through the medium of labor.

The duty of almsgiving is modified by the provision made by the state and by benevolent institutions for the relief of the poor.

The unworthiness and ingratitude of some to whom we may have given aid, does not affect our obligation to bestow alms upon those who are really in want. Our heavenly Father does not withhold from us his daily bounties because we fail to exercise suitable gratitude.

One of the best methods of aiding the necessitous, is to help them to help themselves. To put one in the way of supplying his own wants is far better for him, than to supply his wants without requiring from him any exertion.

It is our duty to instruct the ignorant and to endeavor to reclaim the erring. To benefit the soul is a greater work than to benefit the body. In fact, the former includes the latter. Make an ignorant and vicious man intelligent and moral, and you furnish the conditions of improvement with reference to his outward estate.

Experience has shown that to bring individuals and communities under the controlling influence of religious principle is the most efficient means of promoting their happiness and prosperity. We have seen intemperate and otherwise immoral men transformed into virtuous and useful citizens by the power of the gospel. We have seen communities and nations rescued from degradation and misery by the same power. Witness the changes wrought in the condition of the inhabitants of some of the Islands of the Pacific through the teaching of Christian missionaries.

The law of benevolence requires us to do good to those who hate us. The reason of this lies partly in the fact that such a course has a greater tendency to disarm hatred than has force. The conquests of Christ's kingdom over evil are always conquests of love.

It is our duty to love our enemies,—that is, we should be free from all malignant feelings towards them, and should desire to see them delivered from their enmity and made happy. It is not required that we look upon their characters and conduct with complacency. It is not required that we love them as we love the virtuous and lovely. It is required that we cherish towards them a compassionate, forgiving, benevolent spirit. It is required that we follow the benevolent example of the Saviour.

Benevolence requires us to practice self-denial for the sake of others. In order to do good to others, it is often necessary to deny ourselves enjoyments which would otherwise be lawful.

Nature prompts parents to practice self-denial for the sake of their children. The friend often delights to deny himself for the sake of his friend. There is thus in the structure of the mind provision for self-denial.

When we see a man foregoing some innocent indulgence, or voluntarily enduring suffering that he may relieve the suffering of others, we approve and admire the act. We regard it as a highly virtuous act. Now man was made to perform highly virtuous acts ; hence he was made to practice self-denial.

Christ said, "If any man will come after me, let him deny himself, and take up his cross and follow me." Matt., xvi. 24.

It is a mistake to suppose that self-denial interferes with or lessens our happiness. Those are the happiest who do the most towards making others happy. The most self-denying men are the happiest of men. The self-denial practiced must be the self-denial required by duty, not the self-denial of asceticism.

The amount of self-denial which one may be required to practice, must be determined by the circumstances in which he is placed. Let it be observed, that to abstain from doing wrong, is not to practice the self-denial of which we are treating.

The law of benevolence requires us to cultivate a cheerful disposition. Cheerfulness promotes the happiness of those with whom we associate. Cheerfulness is like sunshine. We have all known men whose presence was everywhere welcome, on account of their cheerful spirit and cheerful countenances.

A gloomy, desponding man throws a chill over every circle that he enters. The happiness of a family may be greatly impaired by a want of cheerfulness on the part of a single member.

If, then, it is our duty to endeavor to make others happy, it is our duty to cultivate a cheerful spirit.

This is done, in the first place, by keeping a good conscience. No one can be cheerful while suffering from remorse. Then, if desponding thoughts enter the mind, they can be banished by turning our attention to thoughts adapted to introduce cheerful thoughts. The gathering cloud of gloom may also be dispelled by active efforts to do good. The imagination must not be allowed to form gloomy images. Things should be viewed as they are, and right views of God's providential government entertained. No one need be gloomy who has a heavenly Father pledged to supply all his wants, and who has declared that all things shall work together for his good. Rom., viii. 28.

Benevolence requires us to cultivate kind and courteous manners. Many upright and kind-hearted men give pain by their unrefined and uncourteous manners. It will not do to say, if the feeling is right, the manner is of no consequence. Our duty is to have kind feelings, and to give to them their appropriate expression. We cannot do our duty to others by having kind feelings, and keeping them perfectly concealed—giving no expression to them. Neither can we do our duty by having kind feelings, and giving to them a very imperfect expression. We do our duty when we have right feelings rightly expressed. The apostolic injunction is "Be courteous." 1 Pet. iii. 8.

God has given to man dominion over the brute creation. That authority should be exercised in accordance with the laws of his moral nature. That dominion was given for certain ends, and it may not be exercised with reference to other ends. It was not given for the exercise of cruelty; therefore he may not treat brutes with cruelty.

Some portions of the animal creation may be used for food. Their lives should be rendered as comfortable and their death compassed with as little pain as possible.

Some animals are given us as servants. They should be treated kindly. As they are not moral beings, they are not the proper subjects of rewards or punishment. Such severity may be practiced as is necessary to keep them in due subjection. To visit on them the outbursts of anger, in consequence of their following the promptings of their nature, is cruelly unjust. The fearful cruelty practiced on the brute creation is an awful exhibition of human depravity, and one of the mysteries of the divine government.

Noxious animals may be lawfully destroyed; but on what principle may harmless ones be destroyed for mere amusement?

CHAPTER XII.

DUTIES OF JUSTICE—RIGHT OF PROPERTY—SELLERS AND BUYERS.

It is our duty to be just to our fellow-men. That we ought to act justly is a proposition that needs no proof. That justice ought to be done is a self-evident truth.

Justice requires us to respect the right of property. We have seen in a former chapter, that the desire of property is natural to man—that God gave man this desire, and placed him amid circumstances favorable to its gratification. Man was, therefore, designed by his Maker to be a holder of property—has a right to hold property.

Men may become lawfully possessed of property in various ways. That which is wholly the product of a man's own labor belongs to him. Men may thus acquire a right to property by labor. The law secures this right, but does not originate it. The right existed previous to any human law. This right may be modified by the law. For example, the law may prescribe the mode in which the right shall be exercised, and the mode in which it may be transferred to another.

Property may be acquired by appropriation, which is only a form of labor. The fruit growing on an uninhabited island belongs to those who may see fit to gather it. Before it was gathered, it belonged to no one. It becomes property by the act of appropriation. The fish in the ocean do not belong to the human family collectively. Before they are caught, they belong to no one. When caught, they are the property of the captor. The act of appropriation is not valid, when exercised upon objects that have been previously appropriated and not abandoned.

Property may be acquired by purchase, that is, one may exchange the products of his labor for the products of the labor of another ; by gift and by inheritance.

The right of property may be violated by robbery, theft and fraud. The duty of avoiding robbery and theft need not be insisted on in this treatise. No one claiming to be a moral man ever contended for the right to rob and steal. Nor has any one ever defended the lawfulness of fraud. Yet there are modes of fraud sometimes practiced and defended by those who profess to do right. Frauds most frequently take place in the operations of buying and selling.

It is the duty of the seller to make known to the purchaser the real quality and condition of the article offered for sale. If he sells a damaged article as a good one, he of course defrauds the purchaser. If he preserves silence in regard to the article, the transaction is still a fraudulent one. He may say, "I did not recommend the article ; I did not say it was not damaged ; the purchaser had it before him ; he was not compelled or urged to buy it ; if he has not got what he wanted it is his own fault :" all this will not lessen his guilt. The sale was a fraudulent one.

It is the duty of the seller not to take advantage of a man's ignorance, and sell him an article less valuable than the one called for. It often happens that the purchaser is not a judge of the goods he is about to purchase. He designs to purchase the first quality but is unable to distinguish the first from the second. If the seller takes advantage of his ignorance, and sells him the second for the first quality, he cheats him to the amount of the difference in value between the first and second.

The seller has no right to sell adulterated articles knowing them to be such, when the buyer thinks they are pure.

As a matter of fact, the adulterating process is carried on very extensively. Some articles can rarely be obtained pure. In consequence of the wide prevalence of the practice, many do wrong without any compunctions of conscience. Nevertheless, when a man calls for ground pepper, and receives a mixture of pepper and buckwheat bran, he is defrauded. It is no excuse for the seller to say that the custom of selling adulterated goods is well nigh universal. The universality of a fact does not change its moral character.

The seller has no right to take advantage of the necessities of the buyer, and, in consequence, to exact a higher price for the goods sold. In such cases the buyer consents to give the price asked under compulsion, just as the traveller consents to part with his purse to the highwayman.

The seller is under obligation to have exact weights and measures, and to know that the quantity sold is actually delivered to the buyer. If the weight or measure fall short, he cannot excuse himself by saying, "I bought it for that amount." The buyer has a right to demand the quantity paid for.

The seller has no right to make a false impression upon the mind of the buyer in regard to the condition of the market. It is possible for him to do this without making any false statement, and the buyer may be thereby led to purchase to his disadvantage. If he is led to believe there is a scarcity in the market when there is not, his action may be quite different from what it would otherwise have been.

A man of large means may not secure a monopoly in regard to a certain commodity, in order to raise the price higher than it would be if there was a competition of sellers. A man has a right to purchase as much of any commodity in market as he chooses. The rectitude of his conduct depends upon the use which he makes of the commodity purchased. If after having purchased all the market contained, he exacts a higher price than the article would command in a fair market, he takes advantage of a necessity created by his own voluntary act. This is especially the case if the article in question be one of the necessaries of life. If it be not one of the necessaries of life, and men choose to purchase it at his enhanced price, he has taken advantage of his capital to realize a higher profit than could be realized by the ordinary modes of trade. If this be not absolutely wrong, it is, at least, ungenerous towards those of lesser means.

Suppose a merchant imports an article on which he realizes a very high profit, in consequence of the fact that no other person imports the article. He enjoys a monopoly of it. Suppose another merchant imports the article and that the former then sells the article at a price lower than it cost to import it—his previous high profits enabling him to do so. He thus destroys the value of the property of his rival in order to preserve his monopoly. It is said that some claiming to be honorable men pursue the course thus indicated.

Suppose a man runs a stage-coach between certain places. He has, for the time being, the monopoly of the business of transporting passengers. By and by, another person procures a coach and proposes to carry passengers. The monopolist, in order to preserve his monopoly, goes and destroys the new coach. His conduct could not be defended. Wherein does the conduct of the importer above supposed differ in principle from that of the stage-coach proprietor?

If a merchant have goods in his possession, and the price of the same rises in the market, he is justified in advancing his price in proportion to the rise. If the price falls, he must make a corresponding deduction, even if by so doing he should suffer loss.

Suppose a merchant has an article for sale, and he knows that on the morrow a large quantity of the article will reach the market and reduce the price. Is he at liberty to conceal his knowledge and sell at the market price of the day? If he put his customers in possession of his knowledge, they would not buy but wait for the certain fall in price. Is he under obligation to communicate his knowledge, or may he reap the advantage of it? May the advantage be regarded as the legitimate reward of his superior enterprise and skill in acquiring knowledge in advance of others?

It would certainly be wrong for him to avail himself of that knowledge, if he had taken any measures to prevent his customers from acquiring it. If he has not done so, is he not entitled to the benefit resulting from his superior activity and enterprise? It certainly cannot be the duty of the industrious and skillful man to share equally with the indolent and stupid the advantages of his industry and skill.

The duties of the buyer correspond to those of the seller. It is his duty to pay a fair price for the article bought, that is, to allow the seller to make a fair profit as a compensation for the use of his capital and for his skill. He has a right to buy where he can buy the cheapest; but he has no right to endeavor to get an article below its real value. He has no right to deceive the seller as to the state of the market, so as to induce him to lower his price.

The buyer has no right to take advantage of the necessity of the seller. The latter may be under the necessity of raising a certain sum of money by the sale of goods by a certain time. The former knowing this, may decline purchasing, except at a ruinous sacrifice on the part of the owner.

It is not, in all cases, wrong to purchase goods below their actual value. When there is no fraud in the transaction, when there is no advantage taken of the seller's necessity, and when goods are lawfully sold by auction, there is nothing wrong in buying them at a price less than their cost or value.

CHAPTER XIII.

DUTIES OF THE EMPLOYER AND EMPLOYED.

The relation of employer and employed is an important one, and lies at the foundation of important and interesting duties. It was formerly designated by the terms master and servant; but those terms have become distasteful to many, partly in consequence of the existence of slavery in the country. The relation must exist as long as society exists.

The employer should treat the employed with exact justice. In making the contract, he should engage to render a full equivalent for the services required, or, in other words, fair wages. He must not take advantage of the ignorance or the necessities of the laborer, and secure his services for less than their market value.

The rate of wages in a community will be determined by the wants and means of employers, and the number of candidates for employment. The matter will, in a great measure, regulate itself. It will do so effectually, if there is no selfish and unprincipled interference with the natural course of things. As things are, the lowest possible wages that will secure labor is not always the wages that should be paid, that is, the actual rates are not always the equitable rates. The principle laid down by Christ, that the laborer is worthy of his hire, should be remembered by every employer.

A distinguished American jurist remarks : "The true rule is, a fair day's wages for a fair day's work ; and those wages are not fair unless they will support the honest and virtuous laborer in comfort, and leave something for the contingencies of life. The practice of putting down labor to a starvation rate, in order to enable the employer to undersell a competitor, is wrong, and will justify a rising feeling of discontent and injustice in the bosom of the employed. Unless such a rule is held sacred, labor must become reckless, vicious, and degraded ; one of the most fearful results for a country with a dense population and overgrown towns and cities. There will grow up feelings of hatred in the bosom of the toiling many against the affluent few. There will justly seem to their minds something wrong in an arrangement which compels them to create wealth for the ease and indulgence of others, while they themselves are starving or suffering. There is, then, a law of proportion between capital and labor, which ought sacredly to be respected, and cannot be violated with safety, nor with impunity. A consciousness of injustice in the minds of the many is a terrible thing. Injustice cannot last always ; God will not permit it ; man will not permit it.

"Cheap goods are not the chief end of man ; nor is free competition the law of salvation for humanity. A thing is worth what it cost to make it, on the principle of paying labor a fair day's wages for a fair day's work, and capital a fair return. It is a sin to sell or buy at a less price.

"Let justice then enter the soul of him who employs his fellow men ; let him so manage that they too shall have their fair wages, time and means to cultivate their moral powers, to become enlightened and virtuous and saving ; so that employer and employed may work together for noble ends by noble means. Such a relation between capital and labor cannot but develop the noblest qualities, and the purest emotions of both ; esteem, and confidence, and love would form the bonds of union between them ; and both would become better, and purer, and holier, by this divine union between capital and labor ;—a union certain in the future, if humanity should ever become developed in its noblest capacities, and indispensable to the safety of capital itself, as well as to the well-being and dignity of the laborer."*

The employer should exact no more labor than is consistent with the health and well-being of the labo-

* Nash's Morality and the State.

rer. The brute may be required to labor all the time except that which is necessary for physical rest. But man is not a brute. He has intellectual, social and moral wants to provide for. He has a right to be a man, and hence a right to the time necessary to that end. When required to devote all his time to labor except that which is necessarily devoted to repose, he is deprived of his rights. There may be times and circumstances when it may be right for the employer to require those in his employment, thus to labor; but, as a general rule, every one is entitled to a portion of his time to devote to higher objects than physical labor.

The employer has no right to interfere with the exercise of the free will of the employed in relation to matters not included in the contract, and not conflicting with the law of right. He has no right to dictate where he shall make his purchases, how he shall vote, or what form of religious worship he shall adopt.

Employers have no right to form combinations for controlling the rate of wages. Large capitalists possess great facilities for so doing. If such combinations are ever justifiable, it is when formed to resist the combinations of laborers to secure higher wages. Combinations of both kinds have an injurious influence and are wrong. Capitalists have greater facilities for secret combinations than laborers have.

The employer should exercise kindness towards

the employed. The law of benevolence written on the heart, and on the pages of the Bible applies first to those with whom we are most nearly connected. The toil of the laborer can be sweetened by the sympathy of his employer. His burden may be lightened by acts of kindness easily performed. The fact that such acts may not always be appreciated is no reason for their not being performed. Our obligation to practice benevolence is not found in man's capacity for gratitude.

Those employed should faithfully fulfil their contract with their employer. A contract to perform a certain amount of labor is as binding as a contract to deliver a certain amount of goods. The employer has a right to claim a certain amount of labor. The employed does not contract to give his time—but his time faithfully devoted to labor.

The employed should cherish a regard for the interest of his employer, and should not content himself with a literal fulfilment of his contract. It is his interest that his employer should be prosperous. All laborers have an interest in the prosperity of capitalists. The greater the prosperity of capitalists, that is, the greater the amount of capital, the larger the fund for paying the wages of labor. An increase of capital in a country, the number of laborers remaining the same, will lead to an increase of wages. When the laborer promotes the prosperity of his employer, he pursues a course adapted to promote his own prosperity. Thus the law, "Thou shalt love thy neighbor as thyself," is a maxim of prudence, as well as a law of benevolence. It is binding alike on the employer and the employed. It is not an unreasonable, much less an impossible command. It simply requires that we cherish such an interest in the welfare of others as is adapted to promote our own highest interest and happiness.

It is the duty of laborers to make no pretensions to skill which they do not possess. In many cases, those requiring their labor are not capable of judging whether they possess the requisite skill or not. Their condition is analogous to that of the man who wishes to purchase goods of a certain quality, but is not a judge of the quality. In neither case should the want of capacity be taken advantage of.

The physician should acquire the knowledge and skill necessary to the practice of the healing art. Kindness, sympathy and assiduous attention are important aids to his prescriptions, and hence should be practiced. It is the duty of the physician to merit the confidence of the patient, since confidence is one of the conditions of recovery.

The physician possesses peculiar facilities for exerting a moral influence on his patients. This is one of the talents committed to him, for the exercise of which he will have to render an account.

The lawyer should not undertake a case which he is not competent to manage. He must possess skill enough to do all that he undertakes to do.

The profession of the law, like the law itself, is designed to subserve the ends of justice. It should not be perverted to the perpetration of injustice.

The lawyer may undertake the defence of one charged with crime, but to the end that he suffer no injustice, not that he may escape without punishment if he is guilty. The lawyer is sworn to prove true to the interests of his client; but not at the expense of truth and justice.

The professional laborer is not bound to follow the instructions of his employer. The physician is not to ask the patient what medicines he shall give. The lawyer is not to ask the client in what manner he shall manage his case. When a matter is committed to a professional agent, he is bound to manage it according to his best ability. Before the matter is committed to him, he may act under instructions.

The teacher should not undertake to do that which he is not qualified to do. Qualifications for the art of teaching are acquired by study and experience, just as qualifications for other arts are acquired. A man is not likely to acquire the qualifications of a teacher while giving all his energies to preparing himself to practice law, any more than a man is likely to acquire the skill of an engraver while devoting himself to the art of making iron. The useful and the fine arts require preparatory study—an apprenticeship. The same is true of the most important of all arts, that of giving "form and pressure" to immortal minds.

If the painter uses the wrong color, he can obliterate it: if the engraver makes an inaccurate line, he can erase it: but impressions made upon the mind are made for eternity. Hence the responsibility of the teacher. Hence the importance of securing for the young mind at the outset, skillful teaching.

The teacher should cherish a deep interest in the welfare of his pupil. His object should not be merely to communicate knowledge but to develop power. He should show his pupil what to do and how to do it. He should strive to make him a seer, and not a mere receptacle of facts. He should aid him in forming proper habits, and in making the mind what the Creator designed it to be.

He should not only possess the knowledge requisite to give information and supervise the studies of his pupils in the department in which he is called to give instruction, but he should possess a character worthy of imitation. Teachers as well as other men influence by what they are more than by what they say.

The pupil should cordially co-operate with the teacher. In many instances the power of the teacher is in a great measure lost through the antagonistic attitude of the pupil. There should be co-operation, respect, affection, that the greatest benefit may result from the relation.

The legislator is a professional agent. He is elected to do a certain kind of work for which he is presumed to possess the requisite skill. Hence he is not to obey the instructions of his constituents or a portion of them, but to act according to his best judgment.

CHAPTER XIV.

PERSONAL LIBERTY—CHARACTER—REPUTATION.

Justice requires us to avoid interfering with the natural liberty of our fellow men. The natural liberty of a man is not liberty to do wrong. He may do as he pleases provided he please to do right. So far as his fellow men are concerned, he is at liberty to do as he pleases provided he does not interfere with their rights. For his conduct in other respects, that is, for his conduct which is in no way injurious to others, he is responsible to God and not to man.

No man may be deprived of this liberty, unless he forfeit it by the commission of crime. Government may, on his being convicted of crime, deprive him of his liberty, but individuals may not do it.

Every man who has not forfeited his liberty by crime, is entitled to the product of his own lawful labor and capital. The government may, if necessary for the public good, take possession of his property, but is under obligation to make compensation for the same. For an individual forcibly to appropriate the product of his labor would be robbery.

God holds every man responsible for what he does. To the end that he might justly hold him responsible, he endowed him with freedom of will. Hence he must be allowed to act according to his own free will, and not be compelled to act according to the will of another. A man may act foolishly or wickedly, but that does not authorize me to compel him to act according to my will instead of his own. I have no right to deprive him of his free agency, because he sees fit to abuse it.

The parent may restrain the liberty of his child, so far as may be necessary for his educational training. It is the exercise of a power which God has bestowed upon the parent for the good of the child.

To restrain the liberty of the idiotic and insane, is not a violation of justice. Justice to others and benevolence to them require restraint in connection with treatment adapted to promote their recovery and comfort.

To restrain the liberty of a prisoner of war, is not a violation of justice. If war is lawful, and with respect to defensive war there can be no doubt, then it is right to take prisoners of war. The right to take prisoners, does not involve the right to deprive them permanently of their freedom. Justice requires that all unnecessary severity be avoided in their treatment.

Justice requires that we do no injury to the

character of others. Character and reputation are distinct. Character is the condition of one's soul. Reputation is the estimation in which one is held by others.

Character includes habits. When a man is forming habits, he is forming his character. The habits which he forms determine his character. As a man's happiness and usefulness depend more upon his character than upon any thing else, injury done to his character is a very serious matter.

We may injure the character of others by our example. If our example leads any one to do wrong, an injury is thereby done to his character, and for that injury we are in a measure responsible. We may not have intended to injure any one, but that does not change the fact or relieve us from the responsibility of an evil example. We are responsible for our influence conscious and unconscious. A large part of our influence is unconscious influence. We influence by what we are—by our characters. Hence our characters should be such as are adapted to exert a healthful influence.

The character may be injured by placing temptations before men, by directly influencing them to do wrong. This is sometimes done in mere thoughtlessness, and sometimes for selfish and malignant purposes.

No greater injury can be done than by leading a

man to violate his conscience, that is, to act contrary to his conscientious convictions of duty. His views may be erroneous, but the effort should be to convince him of his error, not to lead him to act contrary to his moral judgments. It is far better to act in accordance with erroneous moral judgments, than to act contrary to them. Superstitious obedience, is better than defiant opposition to erroneous convictions of duty. The latter tends to the destruction of all moral principle.

It would be regarded as doing one a great injury if we were to deprive him of a limb or an eye ; but this would be doing him far less injury, than to lead him into vice. Injuries done to the body are far less important than injuries done to the soul.

There can scarcely be a baser act than the wilful ruin of a fellow being. Yet such acts are constantly taking place. This appears from the multitudes of unhappy beings who throng at night the thoroughfares of our cities, and revenge upon society the wrong of which they have been the victims.

A powerful means of injury to the character are corrupting books and pictures. Those who issue and circulate such works, cause a ruin that can never be measured. Erroneous arguments can be met by such as are true, but corrupting appeals to the passions cannot be met by argument. Hence the law, very properly, forbids the publication and circulation of corrupting books. Such laws do not interfere with the freedom of the press.

The character may be injured by the inculcation of erroneous moral principles. He who leads another to adopt opinions radically unsound on religious and moral subjects, may do him irreparable injury. His character and conduct will, in a measure, correspond to his principles. Some men are better than their principles, and some are worse; but in all cases, the principles of a man determine the nature of his character. The importance of correct moral and religious principles cannot be too highly estimated.

Justice requires us to avoid injuring the reputation of others. All utterances adapted to injure the reputation of a man are unlawful, unless we are called to bear witness to the truth. A man's reputation, however acquired, is his property, and we have no right to lessen it, simply because we may think it undeserved. If justice to others, if the cause of truth and righteousness require us to make statements, the effect of which may be to damage the reputation of some person or persons, those statements should be made. But they should not be made for the purpose of lessening that reputation, either because we think it greater than it ought to be, or because we are envious of it. Many criticisms claiming to be the utterances of justice, are, in reality, the utterances of envy.

Reputation is often injured through thoughtlessness. A remark may be made or a report repeated, with no design to injure any one's reputation, and yet the injury may be done. Thoughtlessness does not free one from responsibility for his conduct.

We have no right to make public the faults and failings of others, unless required to do so by duty to some individual, or to the public. We have no right to ridicule others; for by thus holding them up to contempt, we injure their reputation and influence.

Slander is the utterance of falsehood respecting another, or the utterance of truth with a malicious intent. It is an act of cruel injustice, and one that is severely punished by municipal law. The evils resulting from this crime are great beyond description. The slanderer is the basest of men.

Slander, in what may be termed its lighter forms, is very prevalent. The criticisms, depreciations, harsh judgments as to motives, which are so abundant, are all forms of slander. God's law in relation to this matter is very explicit. "Thou shalt not bear false witness against thy neighbor." Ex., xx. 16.

CHAPTER XV.

DUTY OF VERACITY.

God has commanded us to speak the truth and lie not. Col., iii. 9. No duty is more insisted on in the Scriptures than reverence for the truth. All agree that lying is not only a vice, but one of the meanest of vices.

It is our duty to speak the exact truth in all our business transactions. In no other way can justice be meted out and honesty preserved. Adherence to the exact truth in all the intercourse of business would put an end to every species of fraud.

It is our duty to speak the exact truth in our ordinary intercourse with men. Some are careful to speak the exact truth in relation to important matters, but are careless as to their statements concerning what they deem unimportant matters. Some, without intending to depart from the truth, fall into habits of exaggeration, and of coloring their statements highly, for sake of effect. Their motive is not to deceive, but to make their conversation interesting. But such habits ought to be carefully avoided. The truth is too sacred a matter to be trifled with. Those who thus trifle with it, soon become careless in their statements in regard to important matters. They fail to discriminate clearly between the true and the false. They lose the confidence of their acquaintances. They are not regarded as men who intend to deceive ; but they are regarded as men whose statements are not to be relied upon. This is certainly a very undesirable reputation.

Our duty is to speak the truth at all times, just as it is our duty to be honest at all times. He who is honest in all large business transactions, but, through carelessness or design, cheats in small matters, cannot be regarded as a perfectly honest man. To be a perfectly honest man, he must be honest in all his transactions, however small, and in order to be a perfectly truthful man, he must speak the truth in regard to all matters, great and small. There are not as many perfectly truthful men as there ought to be.

A falsehood or lie is the utterance of an untruth with the intention to deceive. A fictitious narrative, written or spoken either for amusement or as a vehicle for the communication of truth, is not a falsehood. There is no intention to deceive. Indeed, fiction may convey truth in the most impressive way. Fiction may be the intensest truth. The lawfulness and wisdom of using fiction as the means of conveying and enforcing truth, is sanctioned by the highest possible authority, that of the Lord Jesus Christ. He spake in parables. A parable is a fictitious narrative employed for communicating truth.

A statement may be strictly true, and yet the utterer may be guilty of falsehood. His intention may be to deceive. The statement may be verbally true, but with respect to the meaning intended to be conveyed, or the impression intended to be made, it may be false. The moral character of an utterance depends mainly upon the intention of the utterer.

Falsehood may be committed by silence, or rather by omitting to say what is necessary to the full understanding of the matter in hand. A witness may make no statement but what is perfectly correct, and yet, by omitting a circumstance, his testimony may make an impression entirely adverse to the interests of truth and justice. Hence the oath administered to a witness requires him to tell the whole truth.

A falsehood may be acted as well as spoken. When by a movement of the limbs, or a look, with the intention to deceive, a false impression has been made upon the mind of any one, falsehood has been committed, as really as if the false impression had been made by spoken or written words.

Is a deviation from the truth—the utterance of a falsehood ever justifiable?

Suppose a man asks for information which he has no right to ask for, and which it will do harm for you to communicate. Suppose, for example, he asks for information which, if received, will enable him to injure an innocent person. Suppose that in declining to answer, you really give him the information that he wants, Have you a right to deceive him? Have you a right to give him a false answer?

In war, has a general, fighting in a just cause, a right to deceive his enemy? Has he a right to convey false information to the enemy?

The answer in both of these cases would rest upon the same principle. Has misinformation given in such circumstances the character of falsehood any more than the shooting of an assassin who attacks you has the character of murder? Is not the act as far removed from a voluntary act of deception, as a blow in self-defence is removed from the malice prepense of murder?

Acting in this manner is not doing evil that good may come—a principle condemned by conscience and the word of God. It is not a voluntary departure from the truth. It may be said, "You can speak the truth; you can give the information demanded, and take the consequences? So you may refrain from lifting your hand in self-defence, when the assassin assails you, and may take the consequences. The question is, whether in either case you are under obligation to allow those consequences to follow.

When on a certain occasion the Pharisees asked Christ a question designed to bring him into trouble, he stooped down and wrote on the ground as *though he heard them not.* And when they continued asking him, he gave them an evasive answer. This would, at least, indicate that we are not bound to answer questions having for their design injury to ourselves or others, in the same way that we are bound to answer legitimate questions.

Lying is regarded by men as one of the meanest of vices. To call in question one's veracity is a grievous offence. And yet the precautions men take against deception indicate to what extent habits of truthfulness are wanting in the community.

Young persons sometimes justify the practice of falsehood on the ground of duty to their associates. A fellow student, for example, is guilty of some act that would subject him to censure or punishment. His friend, in order to screen him, bears false witness in his behalf. He regards it as an honorable act to lie.

To refuse to testify against an associate, is different from bearing false witness in his favor. Whether in a given case one has a right to refuse to testify, depends upon the engagement he may have formed with the party requiring the testimony, and the circumstances in which he is placed. One cannot be placed in circumstances which shall make it right for him to do wrong.

CHAPTER XVI.

PROMISES AND OATHS.

All promises are to be faithfully kept. A distinction between important and unimportant promises ought not to be made, so far as keeping them is concerned. He who fails to keep unimportant promises is on his way towards failing to keep important ones.

To avoid committing this fault, we should not make rash and thoughtless promises. Failure to keep any promise, however trifling, exerts an injurious influence on our character, and tends to injure our reputation. There is felt a profound respect for a man who always keeps his promises, always does what he says he will do. It is in the power of every one to command this respect.

Promises are always to be honestly kept. There is such a thing as keeping a promise to the ear and breaking it to the heart. A promise is to be performed in the sense in which it was understood by the person to whom it was made, or at least in the sense in which he had a right to understand it. A person may be so stupid as to misunderstand a clear statement. The promiser is not bound to depart from that statement, because stupidity failed to understand it.

Are promises obtained by fraud binding? Suppose a man tells you he has saved the life of your most intimate friend. In consideration of his supposed conduct, you promise to give him a sum of money on the the morrow. In the mean time, you find that the statement which induced you to make the promise is false. He did not save the life of your friend. He had never seen him. The promise would not be binding. It was in reality a conditional promise, and the condition on his part was not fulfilled.

Is a promise extorted by violence obligatory? Suppose a robber threatens to take your life, and releases you on your promise to send him a certain sum of money: are you under obligation to keep your promise? This case seems to come under the same principle as the question, whether misinformation may be given by an individual, or strategy practiced by a military officer. No rule of universal application can be laid down. There may be cases in which it would be expedient to keep the promise. Paul makes a distinction between lawfulness and expediency. Some things are lawful which are not expedient, and some things may be expedient which are not obligatory. 1 Cor. vi. 12.

Ought a promise to do a wrong thing to be performed? Certainly not. It can never be right to do wrong. If such a promise were obligatory, it would be right to perform it, that is, right to do wrong. If any one finds himself in the position of having promised to do a wrong thing, let him refrain from doing it, and repent of his promise.

When the performance of a promise is impossible the obligation ceases, provided the impossibility was not occasioned by the voluntary act of the party who made the promise. If the want of power to perform was occasioned by the voluntary act of the promiser, the obligation remains.

Contracts are mutual promises between two or more parties. The promises are conditional. The failure of one party to perform the conditions required of him, releases the other party from obligation.

An oath is a solemn promise to tell the truth, with an appeal to God as the witness of our sincerity. The violation of an oath is perjury.

Some regard all judicial oaths as unlawful, because Christ said, "Swear not at all." "Let your communication be yea, yea, and nay, nay; for whatsoever is more than these cometh of evil." Matt., v. 34–37.

Christ forbade profane swearing. That he did not intend to forbid judicial oaths is plain from the fact that he allowed the High Priest to administer to him an oath. "I adjure thee by the Living God," Matt., xxvi. 63, was the Jewish form of putting the oath.

Christ answered to the oath, "Thou sayest it." Again, we have the example of God himself. "For when God made promise to Abraham, because he could swear by no greater, he sware by himself." Heb., vi. 13. Again, "Thou shalt fear the Lord thy God, and serve him, and shalt swear by his name." Deut., vi. 13.

Oaths ought never to be taken without great reverence. They are required too frequently by our laws and on too unimportant occasions. The effect is to lessen the reverence felt for the sanctity of an oath.

Paley remarks that "the levity and frequency with which it is administered, has brought about a general inadvertency to the obligation of oaths, which, both in a religious and political view, is much to be lamented; and it merits public consideration, whether the requiring oaths on so many frivolous occasions, especially in the customs, and in the qualification for petty offices, has any other effect than to make them cheap in the minds of the people. A pound of tea cannot travel regularly from the ship to the consumer, without costing half a dozen oaths at least; and the same security for the due discharge of their office—namely, that of an oath—is required from a church warden and an archbishop, from a petty constable and the chief justice of England."

These remarks apply equally well to the regulations respecting oaths in this country. The sin of irreverence is daily committed by thousands in our land, in connection with the legal administering of oaths.

Those who have conscientious scruples with respecting to taking a judicial oath, are permitted to make an affirmation. A judicial affirmation differs from an oath merely in name. A violation of an affirmation subjects one to the penalties of perjury.

By the common law of England, those who do not believe in God and in a future state of rewards and punishments, are excluded from bearing testimony in courts of justice.

CHAPTER XVII.

ASSOCIATIONS AND CORPORATIONS.

Associations may be formed for purposes consistent with the law of rectitude. No association can be rightfully formed to do that which is wrong, or to do that which it would not be right for an individual to do. Men in their associated capacity often do that which they would not do as individuals, but that is no proof that their conduct is right. Going with the multitude to do evil does not differ in principle, from going alone to do evil.

No man has a right to engage to act toward the members of his association in a manner inconsistent with obedience to the law of the land and the law of God. The rules formed by a voluntary association of men, must not set aside the rules of God.

An association formed for a laudable end, must use lawful means for the attainment of that end. It would be lawful and laudable in certain circumstances, to form an association to promote the ends of justice by the prompt and faithful execution of the laws, but it would not be lawful to form an association to promote the ends of justice by violations of law. The temporary or the permanent good which has seemed to follow the acts of such associations, do not justify their disobedience to law. Vigilance committees and all associations proposing to take the execution of the laws out of the hands of its regularly appointed ministers, are wrong. It is possible, indeed, that the ministers of the law may become wholly unfaithful to their trust and may use their power to protect the guilty and injure the innocent. In such cases, the law of self-defence may justify resistance to the perjured minister of the law. This would be having recourse to the right of revolution.

When associations receive, by the action of the government, a legal personality, they are termed corporations. The formation of corporations is lawful. They form a convenient mode of employing capital, and may be useful in accomplishing that which would not be undertaken by individual enterprise. It is scarcely necessary to say, that men do not cease to become free moral agents by their connection with a corporation, and hence cannot lay aside any of their moral obligations.

The acts of a corporation are the acts of those who compose it—of its members. The power of a corporation is wielded by a majority of its members, but the acts of the majority are binding upon all. The moral responsibility of those acts rests upon all.

A distinction is to be made. If a majority vote to pursue a dishonest course, and the minority, earnestly oppose that course, they are not guilty of dishonesty in the same sense in which the majority are guilty. Still, they are responsible for the acts of the corporation. So far as those acts are wrong, they are responsible for that wrong.

A stockholder of a company that pursues immoral and dishonest courses may not say, "It is contrary to my wishes and my vote, but I cannot help it, therefore I am not to blame for it." He can, at least, help being connected with a dishonest company.

Suppose three men form a partnership for carrying on the manufacture of cotton. Suppose that two of them in opposition to the wishes of the other, practice fraud in conducting the business. Will it do for the honest man to say, "It is done in opposition to my wishes and efforts, and I am therefore not responsible for it." Every one knows that he is responsible for the acts of the firm. When he receives his dividends, he receives in part, at least, the wages of iniquity. Wherein would his conduct differ in principle from those who receive dividends of corporations who violate the sabbath, or make gains by unlawful means?

Men, that is, some men, are apt to lose their sense of moral responsibility when acting in an associated capacity. The maxim "corporations have no souls" doubtless originated in the fact that men acting as members of a corporation, sometimes seem to lay aside their moral characters—seem to abandon those principles to which they strictly adhere in their individual transactions.

Those entrusted with the management of corporate funds should exercise, at least, the same care and economy which they would exercise if they were their own. By this it is not meant that they are at liberty to use them as they would use their own. A man may bestow his own funds in charity, or he may pay a friend higher wages than others pay. He who is entrusted with funds for a certain object, must with all fidelity devote them to that object.

If this rule were adhered to, the cost of operations carried on by corporations and by the government, would not exceed that of operations carried on by individuals. Every one knows that the affairs of a company and of the government, are rarely managed as economically as the affairs of individuals.

CHAPTER XVIII.

DUTIES OF CITIZENS.

MAN was not created a solitary being. He was made to live in society. It is only in a social state that his various powers find occasions for development and room for exercise. Every one is born a member of some state and a subject of some government. He who is born in England (of English parents) is born subject to the constitution and laws of England, and he who is born in the United States, is born subject to the constitution and laws of the United States. The duties of men as members of the state, that is, as citizens, are very important, and should be accurately known.

The state consists of all the population of the country regarded as a body politic. The government is the agency by which the state exercises its power. Government is not the state, but the instrument of the state.

It is the duty of the members of the state, that is, of all citizens, to entertain right views in relation to government. If men have erroneous views in regard to the origin, nature and powers of government, they will have erroneous views of duty with respect to it.

Government is an institution of God—is of divine origin. It is God's will that men should have government. He has ordained that governments shall exist wherever men exist. This appears from the following facts. He has created men with a social nature. That nature renders it necessary for them to live in society. In order that they may live in society, the law of justice must be observed. They must be just to each other. If all men were perfectly just, government as a protecting and restraining power would not be necessary. But we know that all men are not just. Hence there must be a power to protect men in the enjoyment of their rights, and to restrain them from trespassing upon the rights of others. Such a power is Government. Government is necessary to the existence of society.

The Bible recognizes the divine origin of government, and the divine authority of magistrates. "The powers that be are ordained of God. Whosoever therefore resisteth the power, resisteth the ordinance of God." Rom., xiii. 2. This does not teach that the tyrannical usurper of the powers of government has the divine sanction for his conduct. It teaches that the ordinance of government is from God, and that obedience is due to its commands as such. Men may pervert and abuse the institution of government; but its divine authority is not communicated to its perversions and abuses.

If government is an institution of God, then men should administer it according to his will.

The church is an institution of God. Men have no right to use it as a means of accomplishing their selfish purposes. Neither have they a right to use the institution of government as a means of accomplishing their selfish purposes. It should be recognized as God's institution and should be administered according to his will.

When a people are called upon to form a new government, they should have regard to God's will in so doing. It is his will that perfect justice should prevail in a community. The object of government is to secure justice. It is therefore his will that such a form of government should be established as will best secure justice to its subjects.

Some seem to think that governments are wholly the work of men—that they can make or unmake them when and as they please. From what has been said above, it will be seen that this view is erroneous. Government is not an optional matter, any more than conscience is a optional matter.

We are moral beings. All our voluntary acts have a moral character—are either right or wrong. They all ought to be right. In all our actions, we are to have reference to the will of God. "Whether, therefore, ye eat or drink, or whatsoever ye do, do all to the glory of God." 1 Cor., x. 31. If in all our actions we are to have reference to the will of God, we of course must have reference to his will in those relating to government.

The people of every country are under obligation to have the best government possible. They are not at liberty to live under a bad government, because they choose to. They have no right to choose to live under a bad government. It is not God's will that bad governments should exist.

If it is the duty of the people of a country to have the best possible government, then it is the duty of each one of the people to do all in his power towards securing such a government. The people determine the form and character of the government. Whatever is obligatory on the people is obligatory on the individuals comprising the people. Hence no one may say, "I will attend to my own business, and let government matters alone. Those may manage them who choose to."

No one can thus throw off his responsibility. Matters pertaining to government are among the most important ones connected with the interests of this life. A good government is necessary to national prosperity—to intellectual and moral progress.

It is, therefore, our duty to reverence government as an institution of God, and respect magistrates as his ministers. The apostle declares that they are his ministers. Rom., xiii. 6.

Respect for magistrates is a duty too much neglected at the present day. The people are accustomed to look upon magistrates as their own creatures —as deriving all their authority from them. Whereas the power is ordained of God, and the people simply designate those who shall wield that power. The frequent elevation of incompetent and unworthy men to office, has had a tendency to lessen the respect for magistrates.

In other countries, magistrates are surrounded with imposing forms and ceremonies intended to impress the people with respect. These have been dispensed with in our country. Our respect, therefore, must be the result of right views of the nature of government as ordained of God. The magistrate may be worthy of personal respect. When this is the case, it will be rendered him. But if the magistrate should not be worthy of personal respect, yet we should treat him with respect, in consequence of the office. His faults should not be exaggerated ; nor indeed should they be spoken of, unless it be necessary to the public good. The abuse of magistrates tends to lessen our respect for government, and to weaken its power.

It is our duty to cherish respect for the forms of law. Impatience of forms has become characteristic of the American people. And yet there is an important connection between forms and reality. Let the forms of religion be neglected, and the spirit will decay. Let the forms of liberty be abolished, and liberty itself will take its departure. Let the forms of justice be dispensed with, and the reality will soon be found wanting.

Adherence to established forms of enacting, interpreting, and executing laws, may sometimes interfere with the prompt administration of justice; but departure from those forms will infallibly be followed by many instances of injustice. Temporary inconveniences are better than permanent evils.

It is the duty of all citizens to render a prompt and willing obedience to the laws of the land. They are to obey the laws, not because it is prudent and profitable to do so, but because it is right. If government is of God, its commands have the authority of its Author. The teaching of the Scriptures is explicit on this subject. "Put them in mind to be subject to principalities and powers, to obey magistrates." Titus, iii. 1.

The rule here laid down does not sanction the doctrine of passive obedience and non-resistance insisted on by tyrants and the sycophants of tyrants, in other days. It teaches obedience and submission to all just authority.

There are limitations to our obedience. Suppose

the government requires of us that which is plainly beyond our powers: suppose it requires us to work a miracle, or to believe a proposition without evidence. It would not be our duty to obey; because it would not be possible. To punish us for disobedience would be wrong. If it should command us to do something lawful and within our power, and we wilfully destroy our power to do the act required, we could be justly punished.

When the law is in conflict with the law of God, it is not our duty to obey. "We ought to obey God rather than men." Acts, v. 29. God's law is always right. It is our duty always to do right. Hence we are not to do what is contrary to the will of God.

We cannot throw the responsibility of our wrong-doing on the government. "So then every one of us shall give account of himself unto God." Rom., xiv. 12. In giving that account, it will not do to attempt to excuse a transgression of the law of God, by pleading that it was done in obedience to the commands of men.

There are some who have taught that in civil matters the law of the land is to be our rule of action—that whatever the law prescribes, it is right for us to do. Suppose the law should command us to worship idols, or blaspheme God! would it be right for us to obey?

Government may make things in themselves indifferent obligatory, but government cannot change moral distinctions. The color of my garments is a matter of indifference; but if the government should command me to wear clothes of a certain color, I should be under obligation to obey. There would be no conflict between such a law and the law of God.

If the government should command me to believe a certain religious creed, and to worship God according to a certain form, it would transcend its powers. It can rightfully command me to do whatever is just towards my fellow men, but it has nothing to do with my personal relations to God. Hence the Church and the State should never be united. They have different objects and different spheres of action.

While they should not be united, they should be in harmony, not in antagonism. The Church should give its moral support to the State, and the State should secure the rights of the Church. As both are God's institutions, their legitimate workings must be in harmony.

When governments command that which is contrary to the will of God, they are not to be obeyed. But it does not follow that the execution of the law is to be resisted. Suppose the government should command you to give a part of your property for the support of idolatry. It would not be your duty to obey. The government may send its officers to seize your property. It would not be right for you to make forcible resistance—to shoot down the officers, as in case of an attempt at private robbery. It may be your duty to submit to the spoiling of your goods. It is the duty of all to yield a passive submission to the government, till the oppression becomes so great as to justify a resort to revolution.

It is impossible to say when a revolution—that is, the forcible overthrow of an old government, and the establishment of a new one, is justifiable. A single unjust law does not justify the overthrow of the government. If it did, no government would be secure. Unless a law is perfectly wise, it may have some unjust influence somewhere in its operation. As few laws are perfectly wise, so few are perfectly just. To require a human government to be perfect, as a condition of obedience, would be to do away with all obedience.

There is a right of revolution. There are times when it is right for the people to overthrow by force the existing government. In order to this, the oppression and injustice must be great, and the prospect of success good. Unsuccessful attempts to overthrow tyrannical governments have usually been followed with greater sufferings than those which caused the attempts.

It may thus be the duty of the people to submit to a tyrant—to obey the commands of an usurper. This duty is not founded on his right to command;

for he has no such right, but on the principle that the worst kind of government is better than no government, and that submission would be followed by fewer evils than resistance. In such cases, obedience is a dictate of prudence. It is often our duty to follow the dictates of prudence. The Scriptures enjoin the duty of suffering wrong under peculiar circumstances. We are not always to assert our rights. "For this is thankworthy, if a man for conscience towards God endure grief, suffering wrongfully." 1 Pet. ii. 19.

CHAPTER XIX.

DUTIES OF CITIZENS, CONTINUED.

It is not only our duty to obey the laws, but to assist by our influence and aid, if need be, in their execution. It often happens that a particular law is very unpopular in a given community. Those charged with its execution find their office a difficult one. No citizen has a right to throw any obstructions in the way of the execution of a law, because he may deem it unwise, or because a majority whom he may wish to please are opposed to it. If the law has passed through the constitutional forms—has been legally enacted, and is not contrary to the law of God, it is to be obeyed. Citizens are justified in using all lawful measures to cause its repeal; but while it is a law, it is their duty to obey it, and assist in its execution. To get up such a public sentiment as renders the law a dead letter, differs in form only from forcible resistance to the law. Such a course lessens reverence for the authority of law, and tends to anarchy.

It is the duty of citizens to contribute cheerfully such sums as are necessary for the support of government, in other words, it is their duty to submit to taxation. Taxes are sums levied by the government to defray its expenses and promote the general welfare. A man's taxes are what he pays for the protection of his life and property, and for the conditions of public prosperity in which he shares. He ought to pay his just portion of the expense of government. To endeavor to avoid this, and to throw the burden upon others is unjust and mean.

There is, on the part of some, a want of correct moral perception in relation to this duty. Men who would not defraud others in their ordinary business transactions, who would not make their indebtedness a penny less than justice requires, will make their taxes as small as possible, by not furnishing full information as to their property. The excuse is, that everybody tries to pay as little in taxes as possible.

This excuse is not valid for two reasons. First, it is not true that this course is pursued by every one. There are those who wish to do what is just in regard to taxes, as in regard to other things. They wish to do what is right in all circumstances. In the second place, the fact that another man fails to do his duty, does not justify me in neglecting mine. In case of a contract between two parties, the failure of one to perform his part may absolve the other from obligation to perform his. But there is no analogy between contracts and taxes.

Men should contribute to the expenses of government in proportion to their means. Direct taxes are those that are assessed, or are intended to be assessed, on individuals in proportion to the property possessed by each. It is the most equitable mode of taxation, and yet perfect justice is never reached in the matter. Government in this as in other things is affected by the imperfection of human nature.

Indirect taxes are taxes laid on commodities as they are produced, or sold, or used. The tax is added to the price, and is paid by the consumer of the article. Of indirect taxes, men pay not in proportion to the amount of property possessed, but to the amount of taxed articles consumed by them. The fact that this mode of taxation is less equitable does not justify the attempt to evade the law.

Smuggling is a form of violating the law of taxation. When, as in most cases, there are taxes on goods imported to a country, there are those who seek to import goods without paying the duties. They can undersell those who pay the duties, by reducing the price of their goods. Smuggling is always conducted by unprincipled men. A professional smuggler is not regarded as differing much from the thief and gambler.

It is said that ladies and gentlemen of high social standing sometimes bring into the country, on their persons or in their luggage, articles on which the law requires duties to be paid. The social standing of such travellers may exempt them from suspicion on the part of custom-house officers, but it is difficult to see wherein the moral character of their conduct differs from that of the vulgar smuggler.

Purchasing smuggled goods knowing them to be smuggled, renders the purchaser a participator of the fraud against the government.

It is the duty of citizens to cherish the spirit of patriotism, or the love of their country. The love of country is natural. We are so made that we love first and most intensely the members of our own families, next our more intimate personal friends, next the members of the community in which we live, and next the people of the country to which we belong. Love of our own country is not hatred of other countries. In the family of nations, the interest of one nation is connected with the interest of all other nations. In former times, statesmen thought that they could promote the prosperity of their nation by injuring the prosperity of other nations. Juster views now prevail, and it is clearly seen that it is for the interest of each nation that all other nations should be prosperous.

Our love of country should therefore be shown in honest efforts to promote the prosperity of our own country, not in efforts to lessen the prosperity of other countries. National, like individual selfishness is not wise.

Citizens should endeavor to promote the prosperity of the country by electing competent and honest men to office. The character of the practical operation of our government depends upon the character of those appointed to make, interpret and execute the laws. It rests with the citizens to determine the character of the legislators, judges, and executors of the laws. The exercise of the right of suffrage is one of the most responsible acts of the American citizen. A single vote may determine the policy that may affect the destiny of millions. It is not often that a single vote carries an important election, but it is sometimes the case. Not many years ago, a single vote determined the election for governor in Massachusetts.

The duty of suffrage is violated by those who abstain from voting. It is not an optional matter any more than returning money entrusted to one's care is optional. The right of suffrage is a solemn trust which those to whom it is committed are bound to exercise.

The directors of an insurance company are charged with the management of the affairs of the company. Their duty is to manage it wisely and justly for the benefit of the stockholders. Suppose a majority of the directors are honest men. Suppose they neglect to attend the meetings of the board of directors, neglect to attend to the trust committed to them, and allow the minority to manage the affairs of the company for their own private advantage. Such neglect of duty would be severely censured.

The trust committed to those who possess the power of suffrage is far more important than that committed to the directors of any insurance company. It is of far more consequence that the affairs of the state be wisely and justly managed for the benefit of the state than that the affairs of the company be wisely and justly managed for the benefit of the stockholders. What shall be said of those honest men who neglect to attend elections and allow selfish politicians to manage public affairs for their own advantage?

The duty to exercise the right of voting involves the duty of using the means necessary to render the votes effective. It involves the duty of taking part in those preliminary measures which result in designating the candidates for office.

It is the duty of every citizen to vote for men who are qualified intellectually and morally, for the trust proposed to be conferred upon them. Friendship and self-interest should not influence men to vote for those who are not fully qualified. It is to be feared that votes are often given to candidates merely because they are the candidates of a party.

It is the duty of citizens to cherish a regard for

the public good, and to be willing to put forth efforts, and if need be, to make sacrifices to promote it. To this end it is the duty of every one to promote the cause of intellectual and moral education in the community. Intelligence is necessary to enterprise and a wise direction of industry, and industry lies at the foundation of national prosperity. Besides, an ignorant people are unfit to manage free institutions such as ours. Every patriot should be led by his patriotism as well as by an enlightened regard to his own interest to promote the growth of intelligence among the people.

But intelligence will not of itself secure wise and right action. Men do not perform their duty just in proportion to their knowledge of it. The sense of duty must be strengthened that the duties which intelligence reveals may be performed. Now there is an intimate and inseparable connection between religion and morality. Washington warned the people against the idea that morality could exist without a religious basis.

Hence it is the duty of every citizen to promote the religious education of the community. To promote the circulation of the word of God, and its study, is the duty of the citizen patriot as well as of the christian. "Godliness is profitable unto all things, having the promise of the life that now is, and of that which is to come."

CHAPTER XX.

DUTIES OF LEGISLATORS.

It is the duty of legislators to make wise and just laws. It is hardly necessary to add the word just after wise, for a law that is not just cannot be wise. A man who is not competent to make wise laws has no right to be a legislator. No man can with propriety be said to have a right to do what he does not know how to do. A man cannot claim the right to read Greek till he knows how to read Greek, and no man can claim the right to make laws till he knows how to make laws.

Suppose a man wholly ignorant of the art were to offer himself for employment as a watchmaker! Is watch making more important than law making? Are interests which would be periled by committing the delicate structure of the watch to unskillful hands to be compared with the interests periled by committing the work of legislation to unskillful hands?

Legislators should see that all laws enacted by them are in accordance with the constitution. The constitution is the fundamental law of the land to which all other laws must be conformed. The constitution distributes the powers of government. It gives to the legislature its power. The legislature can make such laws only as the constitution empowers it to make. Laws not in accordance with the constitution have no authority. They will be formally pronounced null and void by the tribunal appointed for that purpose by the constitution.

Legislators must see that the laws enacted by them are according to the law of God. Laws in conflict with the law of God are without authority. We are always to obey the higher law. God's law, the eternal law of rectitude, is the highest law known to the universe. It is the grand constitutional law of the universe, to which all other laws must be conformed.

Legislators should act for the good of the whole country for which they are called to legislate. A legislator may be the representative of a particular community. It is his duty to become acquainted with the condition of that community, and to pay special attention to its interests. He is not, however, to attempt to promote the interests of his constituents at the expense of the interests of the whole country, or of any part of it. He is one of those chosen to make laws for the whole country, and should have paramount regard to the interests of the whole country.

Of course, he should not be influenced by party prejudices. He is in all cases to act according to his own judgment of what is wise and right, and not according to the dictation of the leaders of the party to which he may belong.

Legislators should treat the institutions of religion with respect and reverence. They are bound impartially to protect the rights of all worshippers. They cannot legislate for the conscience. They have no right to punish men for their creed.

In former days, legislators thought they were to legislate for religion. They, therefore, prescribed the doctrines to be believed and the forms of worship to be observed, and punished men if they differed from the creed and practice ordained by the government. The relation of the government to the church is now better understood. Christ's kingdom is not of this world. It seeks no aid from the government in doing its appropriate work. It simply claims the protection due to all the subjects of the state. It gives all its influence to the support of the state acting in its legitimate capacity.

It is the duty of legislators and all other public officers to set an example of propriety of manners and of correctness of moral and religious deportment. When the leaders of a nation are leaders in vice, and a majority of the people are content to have it so, that nation may soon expect punishment at the hand of the Governor of the nations.

The nation is responsible for the acts of its rulers, for they are its agents. If they pursue an unjust and iniquitous course, their sins will be visited upon the nation. There is no truth more clearly asserted in the Bible, and more fully illustrated in history, than that God rewards and punishes nations according to their works. "At what instant I shall speak concerning a nation and concerning a kingdom to pluck up, to pull down, and to destroy it, if that nation against which I have pronounced turn from their evil, I will repent of the evil which I thought to do unto them. And at what instant I shall speak concerning a nation and concerning a kingdom to build and to plant it, if it do evil in my sight that it obey not my voice, then will I repent of the good, wherewith I said I would benefit them." Jer., xviii. 7–10.

The history of the Jewish nation recorded in the Bible is an illustration of the principles here laid down. The history of all past nations is analogous to the history of the Jewish nation.

Nations are rewarded and punished in this world, because they will have no existence in the next. Individual guilt will be the subject of future retribution, but national sins are visited by national judgments in this world.

It may be objected, that the disasters of nations are

the natural consequences of their conduct, and, therefore, not visitations of God. But how came it to pass that disastrous consequences follow one kind of conduct and favorable ones another? Is it not the result of the ordination of God? Is not that which he does by means as truly his work as that which he does without means?

CHAPTER XXI.

DUTIES OF JUDGES.

The office of the judge is to interpret the law. He does not make the law: he decides what the law is in regard to the case in hand.

The welfare of the community is intimately connected with the wise and just interpretation and application of the laws. It is in connection with the decision of the judge that the law comes home "to their business and bosoms." Able and upright judges contribute largely to the public prosperity.

It is the duty of those having the appointing power, to select the ablest and most upright men in the land to act as judges. They should be rendered so far independent of the other departments of the government, and of popular favor, that their decision may be unbiased by considerations of interest.

The judge should be learned in the law and in the rules of interpretation. As the field from whence he is to derive knowledge for his guidance in the discharge of his official duties is ever widening, he should constantly be a diligent student. In other words, he should be constantly increasing his qualifications for the office he holds.

It is the duty of the judge to decide according to the law. He may deem the law unwise, and he may even believe that in the case before him it will work injustice; still he is bound by his oath of office to decide according to the law.

The character of the judge should be one of spotless integrity. The judge is the redresser of wrongs. If he lack integrity, if his decisions are the result of prejudice, or passion and self-interest, a state of things occurs which is thus described by the prophet, "And judgment is turned away backward, and justice standeth afar off; for truth is fallen in the street and equity cannot enter." Isa., lix. 14.

The office of a judge is one of dignity, and those who hold it, should maintain the dignity of the office. To this, a distant and haughty bearing is not necessary, nor the trappings with which the judges of some countries are surrounded. The dignity of the judge should reside in the man, not in his garments.

Jurors are men called upon to act as judges in a particular case. Jurors are judges of the facts of the case. Their business is to listen to the testimony, and give their decision in view of that testimony. They are to receive the instruction of the judge as to the law: they are to decide as to the facts according to the evidence. Suppose a man is on trial for theft.

He is charged with having stolen fruit. A man is called to act as a juror on the trial. He must pronounce the man guilty or not guilty according to the evidence set before him. It may be that he knows that the accused is guilty. It may be that he saw him take the fruit. Still his knowledge must not influence him in making his decision. He must decide according to the evidence. If proof of the man's guilt is not brought forward, he must pronounce him, not guilty.

The juror as well as the judge is bound to decide with fairness and impartiality. All the responsibilities of the judge, so far as justice is concerned, rest upon the juror.

The trial by jury is regarded as one of the greatest safeguards of justice and liberty. Its value depends upon the fidelity with which the jurors exercise their functions. If their verdicts are rendered in accordance with their prejudices, if they regard their obligations to those with whom they may be associated in politics or otherwise as superior to their obligations to do justice, if bribery and corruption enter the jury-box, then the institution may become a curse rather than a blessing.

The judges are required to adhere strictly to the law, and the jurors to the evidence set before them. It may be that false testimony may be brought forward, and thus an innocent man may be declared guilty. Having been pronounced guilty by the jurors, the judge is compelled to pronounce sentence upon him according to law, though he may be perfectly convinced that the prisoner is innocent. Or it may happen that the law may be so constructed that in a given case the judge may be compelled to inflict a penalty exceeding the deserts of the prisoner who has been justly convicted.

In such cases, the pardoning power comes to the aid of justice. The executive is under obligation to pardon all those who would suffer injustice by the due execution of the law.

CHAPTER XXII.

DUTIES OF EXECUTORS OF THE LAWS.

All experience has shown that the security for justice is the greatest when one set of men make the laws, and another administer, them, and another exe-them. Hence it is the duty of the people to make this distribution of the powers of government. They have done so in our government, and a similar distribution has been made in all constitutional governments which have recently been made.

The chief magistrate of a nation or state, whether he is called king, president or governor, is primarily charged with the execution of the laws. He has no right or power to alter the laws, or to set them aside. He cannot interfere with the decisions of the judges. His business is to execute the laws. He is not responsible for the acts of the law makers, nor for the acts of the judges. He is responsible simply for the execution of the laws.

As it is not possible for him in person to execute all the laws, he must appoint subordinates to act under his direction. It is his duty to appoint men of integrity who are competent to do the work assigned them. He is acting for the public and is to have regard only to the public good. He may not bestow offices upon unworthy men as the reward of partisan services. The example of the Father of his country should be followed by all who are invested with the executive power. He sought for men competent to fill the vacant offices. He had regard to services rendered to the country but not to services rendered or promised to himself. He would never have appointed a man who founded his claim on services rendered to the party who elevated him to power.

Those charged with the execution of the laws should be fearless and impartial in the discharge of their duty. They have but one thing to do. They are to carry into execution the decisions of the courts. They are to do what the law explicitly tells them to do.

Security of life and property depends upon the prompt and vigorous execution of the laws. Wise laws are of no avail unless they are enforced.

The chief executive of a nation or state is usually invested with the power to pardon those who have been convicted of crime. It is his duty to use this power for the ends for which it was given him, and for no other.

The pardoning power is given to correct the injustice which a strict adherence to law might sometimes occasion, and to promote the cause of good government.

The executive is not at liberty to exercise it on account of pity for the suffering the execution of the law would occasion, nor because influential men request it. It is to be feared that the increasing frequency with which criminals are pardoned will do much to impair the efficiency of the laws, and to give impunity to fraud and violence. No part of the executive duty should be more carefully and conscientiously performed, than that relating to the exercise of the pardoning power.

It is the duty of the officers of government, and indeed of all men, to cherish right views in regard to the object of punishment. Some assume that the object of punishment is the reformation of the offender: hence, if to pardon him will be more likely to reform him than to execute the sentence, he ought to be pardoned. This false view of the object of punishment has already led to great evils, and threatens to lead to still greater ones.

The primary object of punishment is the meting out of justice. Justice is the fundamental idea of government. All the provisions of government have for their object the maintenance of justice between man and man. Now it is just that crime should be punished. It is a self-evident truth that justice ought to be practiced. It is a self-evident truth that injustice ought to be punished. That crime deserves punishment is assumed throughout the Word of God. A distinction is everywhere made between the righteous and the wicked. The righteous are regarded as worthy of reward, and the wicked of punishment.

The view of punishment above alluded to implies that society is under obligation to do more for the guilty than for the innocent. Abraham, the friend of God, did not so understand the matter; "that the righteous should be as the wicked," that is, have no advantage over the wicked, "that be far from thee. Shall not the judge of all the earth do right?" Gen., xviii. 25.

It may be said, by way of objection, that God punishes guilt for its own sake, but that the prerogative is confined to him—that with man the object of punishment is different.

To this it may be replied, that government is an institution of God, and hence is to be conducted on the principles laid down by him. By the voice of our nature and his written word, he has indicated his will that the guilty shall be punished.

Another object of punishment by government is the security of the law-obeying portion of the people. If no punishments were inflicted, no one will contend that life and property would be secure. Now just so far as punishment fails to be inflicted the security is lessened.

Security of life and property do not depend upon the severity of the punishment so much as upon its certainty. Let it be certain that the penalty attached to a crime will follow its commission; that the offender will be arrested, tried, convicted, sentenced, and the sentence executed, and crime would be almost unknown. It is the duty of the officers of government to see to it that this certainty of punishment follows the commission of crime. Mercy to the criminal is often cruelty to the innocent.

CHAPTER XXIII.

THE DUTY OF REST AND OF PUBLIC WORSHIP.

It is the duty of man to labor. Physical labor is necessary to the development of the bodily powers, and mental labor to the development of the mental powers. Labor, physical and mental, is necessary to produce the necessaries and comforts of life. The duty of labor is thus clearly inferible from the structure of the body and of the mind, in connection with the circumstances in which man is placed.

The Bible teaches the duty of labor. It sets forth the sublimest of examples. "My Father worketh hitherto and I work." Adam was placed in the garden of Eden to till it and dress it. The command from Mount Sinai is, "Six days shalt thou labor,"—not "Six days mayest thou labor." Labor is here spoken of as imperative, not as optional. The Apostle speaking of some who were disorderly and idle, says, "Now them that are such we command and exhort by our Lord Jesus Christ, that with quietness they work, and eat their own bread." 2 Thess., iii. 12. He also commands Christians to "be diligent in business."

There is no exception made in favor of the rich. The rich have no more right to be idle than the poor. A different kind of industry may be incumbent upon them, but every one has or ought to have his own work, which he is to do with his might.

Hence no one has a right to live by the sweat of another's brow, and no one has a right to lead a life of voluntary dependence upon others. The law of labor cannot be violated with impunity.

The body and mind are so constituted that labor must be followed by rest. Rest as well as labor is a duty. It is necessary to the highest efficiency of labor mental and physical. Labor uninterrupted by rest will destroy health and all capacity for labor.

At least one-seventh part of the time should be set apart for rest,—and this in addition to the hours spent each day in taking food, in recreation and in sleep. From a wide examination of facts, it has been found that the physical labor of men and of animals subject to their control is most productive when every seventh day is devoted to rest. At first view, it would seem that more would be accomplished by laboring seven days instead of six, but facts have furnished convincing proof of the assertion above made. This clearly shows it to be the will of the Creator that men should rest one-seventh part of the time.

If it is the duty of all men to rest one day in seven, then it is the duty of all to rest on the same day.

The advantages of rest can in no other way be secured. Men are dependent upon one another. There must be a constant exchange of commodities and services. If the farmer should rest on one day, the mechanic on another, and the merchant on another, exchange and business intercourse between them must cease, or the rest of all must be imperfect. Let all observe the same day of rest, and all these inconveniences will be avoided.

The commandment is in keeping with these deductions of reason. "The seventh day is the sabbath of the Lord thy God: in it thou shalt not do any work, thou, nor thy son, nor thy daughter, thy manservant, nor thy maidservant, nor thy cattle, nor thy stranger that is within thy gates." Ex., xx. 10.

In accordance with the example set by Christians of the apostolic times, the first day of the week according to our mode of reckoning, is observed as a day of rest and of worship throughout Christendom, instead of the seventh.

Exceptions to this law of abstinence from labor relate to works of necessity and mercy. The necessity must not be one voluntarily imposed. We must not confound that which we may strongly desire to do, with that which is necessary.

It is lawful to do good on the sabbath day. The sabbath was made for man. Mark, ii. 27. The object of its institution was his improvement and happiness.

Hence the day of rest is not to be a day of austerity and gloom. It is a day for the reunion of the family, separated, it may be, during the week, by the demands of labor. It should be a day of cheerful enjoyment. It is God's will that the sabbath should be regarded "as a delight." Isa., lviii. 13.

As the sabbath was made for man, that is for his improvement, and especially his moral improvement, such exercises should be held as shall conduce to that improvement, without violating the law relating to labor. One most prominent means of securing this improvement, is that of meeting together for religious instruction and religious worship.

The mere act of meeting together with the decorum suitable for public worship tends to develop our sympathies and promote refinement and courtesy. Our emotions are increased by sympathy, especially our moral emotions. All experience has shown that nothing tends so much to strengthen religious principle and promote religious feeling, as the public worship of God. Where it is not practiced, the community soon becomes immoral and degraded. Where it is strictly and faithfully observed, a virtuous, intelligent, cultivated and prosperous community is the result. The apostle insists on the duty of assembling ourselves together. Heb., x. 25.

The sabbath may be violated by excessive labors to do good. Attendance upon public services to the exhaustion of the body, is not in accordance with the design of the institution.

All worldly amusements are inconsistent with the rest and moral improvement which it is the design of the sabbath to secure.

It is worthy of remark that constitutional liberty has been enjoyed in those countries only in which the sabbath is regarded as a day of rest and of religious worship. Facts show that there is an intimate connection between a reverence for the sabbath and the prosperity of nations.

The government is under obligation to protect its subjects in the enjoyment of the rest of the sabbath, and of worship according to their own convictions of duty. They must not, however, on the plea of conscience interfere with the rest and worship of others. The government should forbid all unnecessary labor on the sabbath. Hence government works should not be continued on that day. It is a national violation of the sabbath for which God will hold the nation accountable.

Let it be remembered that the voice of nature and of Christ unite in declaring that the sabbath was made for man, not for the Jews merely. It is not an institution of Judaism but of human nature. Hence the abolition of Judaism does not affect the sabbath.

The government has no right to enjoin the religious observance of the sabbath. Government has to do with the relations men sustain to each other as members of the state. It can enforce the duties arising from those relations. With man's duties to God as a spiritual worshipper, it has nothing to do by way of enforcement. It can secure to him freedom from interruption in worship, but with the spiritual act it has nothing to do.

Whenever government has attempted to legislate for the conscience, it has inflicted grievous wrongs. Whenever it has attempted to regulate the affairs of the church, it has always corrupted it. The union of church and state has always been fraught with injury to the church.

CHAPTER XXIV.

THE FUTURE LIFE.

If man's existence were confined to this world, he would be none the less a subject of duty; all the duties we have considered would be incumbent on him. He is a subject of duty not because he is immortal, but because he has a moral nature, and sustains certain relations to God and his fellow beings.

Man's existence is not confined to this world. He is to live in another world, and that truth is the foundation of certain duties, or rather modifies all his duties.

The teachings of nature respecting man's immortality are in keeping with the teachings of the Bible; but are not of themselves sufficient to establish it. Nature gives us intimations sufficient to render it probable that there is a future life; revelation is needed to give us assurance. Immortality is brought to light, is rendered an incontrovertible truth, by the gospel.

If there is a future life, and if there is any connection between our conduct here and our condition hereafter, then, as rational beings, we are under obligation to have regard to that future life. If there is merely a probability of a future life, we are under obligation to be influenced by that probability. We constantly act with reference to probabilities. The probabilities of a storm affect the action of the sailor; the probabilities of rain, the haymaker; the probabilities of a future demand for goods, the merchant. And so, if the evidence of a future life amounted to a probability only, we should be under obligation to have regard to that probability in our conduct. Much more when the probability becomes a certainty.

The arguments from nature in favor of the soul's immortality are chiefly negative, and prepare the way for the moral argument, which has great force; but this has for one of its conditions a portion of revealed truth. When we have, by the word of God, been assured of man's immortality, we can trace in nature many intimations which had otherwise escaped our observation.

The argument from analogy is sometimes insisted on as a strong one; but it simply suggests the possibility of the soul's future life. As man exists, previous to birth, in childhood, and in old age, in very different conditions, so he may exist hereafter in a condition very different from those he passes through here.

The different conditions referred to in this life are different stages in the growth of an organized body. At death that body is dissolved into its original elements. The analogy scarcely justifies the inference, that the soul will exist hereafter separate from the body.

This argument is somewhat strengthened when it is rendered highly probable that the death of the body is not the death of the soul. A limb may be cut off, but the mind remains uninjured. A considerable portion of the body, even to a part of the brain, may be destroyed without destroying the soul. It is, therefore, possible, perhaps probable, that the destruction of the whole body will not be the destruction of the soul. The force of this inference is lessened by the fact, that the destruction of certain parts of the body, puts an end at once to all indications of the existence of vital powers, bodily or mental.

The fact that the exercise of the mental powers may be suspended, when they are not destroyed, appears from the phenomena of sleep, and especially of swooning. This fact suggests the possibility that death, though destroying the evidences of the existence of those powers, may not be the destruction of them.

This suggestion receives an increase of probability, when the different parts of the body are viewed as the instruments of the mind. The leg is the instrument of locomotion. Remove the leg, and the mind is not affected. The mind can still perform its part towards the act of walking, as appears from the fact that locomotion can take place through the instrumentality of a wooden leg. The eye is the instrument of seeing and the ear of hearing. The destruction of the eye may not be the destruction of the mind which sees, any more than the destruction of a telescope is the destruction of the mind that has used it.

There are other considerations that might be adduced to show that the death of the body is not necessarily the destruction of the soul. They suggest the possibility, and in the view of some, the probability of the future life of the soul. They remove objections, and prepare the way for the moral argument, which has great force. Let it be granted that man is under a perfect moral government, as he must be, if he is under the government of an infinitely wise, just, and powerful Being, then a future state is seen to be necessary. Men are not rewarded and punished with exact justice here, therefore they will be hereafter. A future life is necessary for this purpose. The argument rests on the fact that there exists an infinitely wise, just, and powerful moral Governor, and this fact nature does not clearly teach. It is taught by revelation, which throughout assumes rather than teaches the immortality of men.

The truth, that man is an immortal being, and

that there is a connection between his conduct here and his condition hereafter, being established, very important duties are brought to light. If it be our duty in youth to prepare for the period of manhood, much more is it our duty to prepare in this life for the life to come.

As no one who has entered the unseen world has returned to give us information concerning that world, we are dependent for our knowledge respecting it, and of consequence our duties in relation to it, wholly on the Bible. The Bible enters into no details respecting the future life. It contains nothing merely adapted to gratify human curiosity. It gives us the knowledge necessary to a knowledge of duty, and no more.

Heaven is represented as the abode of holy beings. A holy, that is, a perfect character, is the preparation for heaven. Without holiness no man shall see the Lord. Heb., xii. 14. Holiness is the sum of perfection. So far as we are striving to form perfect characters, we are striving to prepare for a residence in "the better land." Hence one of the most important modes of preparing for the life to come, is the assiduous performance of the duties of the life that now is.

All the duties of life receive additional importance from their connection with the life to come. Our pursuits and aspirations should be worthy of beings whose existence is to run parallel with the existence of God.

We should have respect to the sublime rewards of eternity. They will nerve us for stronger exertion and lift us to a higher elevation. The Bible does not inculcate a mercenary spirit. It does not found our obligations to obedience on the consequences of obedience or of disobedience. But it authorizes us to have respect "to the recompense of reward" to be bestowed in the future life. "He shall reward every man according to his works." Matt., xvi. 27. It authorizes us to derive from the future life strength to perform difficult duties and endure trials. Christ directed his disciples not only to endure revilings and persecutions for his sake, but to rejoice and be exceeding glad in view of them, "for great is your reward in heaven." Matt., v. 12.

It is our duty and our privilege to look forward to heaven as our home, and to desire it for its rest from painful toil and freedom from sin; for its glorious society, and its endless activities in the service of God.

THE END.

Progressive Higher Arithmetic: combining the Analytic and Synthetic Methods, and forming a complete Treatise on Arithmetical Science, in all its *Commercial* and *Business* Applications, for Schools, Academies and Commercial Colleges.

Particular attention has been given to the preparation of those subjects, which are absolutely essential to make good *accountants* and commercial business men; and among them, Percentage, in its numerous applications to Stock-Jobbing, Brokerage, Insurance, Banking, Averaging Accounts Current, Interest Accounts, Domestic and Foreign Exchange, etc.

Arithmetical Examples. This book has recently been added to the Series, and contains over 1,500 Practical Examples, promiscuously arranged, and without the answers given, involving nearly all the principles and ordinary processes of common arithmetic, designed thoroughly to test the pupil's judgment; to cultivate habits of patient investigation and self-reliance; to test the truth and accuracy of his own processes by proof; in a word, to make him independent of a text-book, and written rules and analyses.

The most noticeable feature of this work will be, the *practical character* of the examples, and the large amount of facts, statistics and information of recent date, which are combined, and form the data in a large proportion of these examples.

This work is not designed for beginners, but for those who have acquired at least a partial knowledge of the theory and applications of numbers from some other work, and it may be used in connection with any other book, or series of books on this subject, for Review or Drill Exercises.

An Edition is printed *exclusively* for *teachers*, containing the answers at the close of the book.

New Elementary Algebra: a clear and practical Treatise adapted to the comprehension of beginners in the Science.

University Algebra. This is the first book the author published on this subject, in 1847, although subsequently enlarged and twice revised. No book of the kind has ever been so favorably received and so enthusiastically admired as this.

There is no *real* necessity for this book in the Series, of which it forms a part, but it may be used by those who do not desire to take so extensive and thoroughly scientific a course as is given in the "New University Algebra."

New University Algebra, containing many new and original Methods and Applications both of Theory and Practice, and is designed for Colleges and High Schools.

This book is not a *revision*, but a newly prepared and recently published work, thoroughly scientific and practical in its discussions and applications. It is a book filled with gems, and most of them original with the author.

New Geometry and Trigonometry, embracing Plane and Solid Geometry, and Plane and Spherical Trigonometry, with numerous practical Problems, the whole newly illustrated.

New Surveying and Navigation. With use of Instruments, essential Elements of Trigonometry, Mensuration, and the necessary Tables, for Schools, Colleges, and Practical Surveyors.

This work is not a *revision*, but an entirely NEW TREATISE, finely illustrated, full and complete, with numerous examples, embodying the most modern and practical methods.

Conic Sections and Analytical Geometry; recently prepared for High Schools and Colleges.

Differential and Integral Calculus. Re-written and enlarged; finely illustrated; in one volume, will be ready April, 1865.

Elementary Astronomy. An Elementary Class-book, in which mathematical demonstrations are omitted.

University Astronomy. Descriptive, Theoretical and Physical, designed for Schools, Academies and Colleges. Large 8vo.

Concise Mathematical Operations. Being a Sequel to the author's Class-books, with much additional matter.

Key to Geometry & Trigonometry, Analytical Geometry & Conic Sections, Surveying & Navigation. With some additional Astronomical Problems. in one volume.

Keys to the Arithmetics and Algebras, are published for the use of Teachers.

www.ingramcontent.com/pod-product-compliance
Lightning Source LLC
LaVergne TN
LVHW011237110826
845150LV00006B/1662

* 9 7 8 1 4 2 5 5 1 3 9 1 7 *